An Introduction to Qualitative Research Synthesis

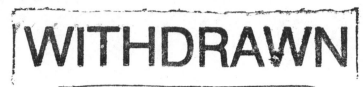

Providing a comprehensive guide for understanding, interpreting and synthesizing qualitative studies, *An Introduction to Qualitative Research Synthesis* shows how data can be collated together effectively to summarize existing bodies of knowledge and to create a more complete picture of findings across different studies.

The authors describe qualitative research synthesis and argue for its use, describing the process of data analysis, synthesis and interpretation, and provide specific details and examples of how the approach works in practice.

This accessible book:

- fully explains the qualitative research synthesis approach;
- provides advice and examples of findings;
- describes the process of establishing credibility in the research process;
- provides annotated examples of the work in process;
- references published examples of the approach across a range of fields.

Helping researchers to understand, make meaning and synthesize a wide variety of datasets, this book is broad in scope yet practical in approach. It will be beneficial to those working in social science disciplines, including researchers, teachers, students and policymakers. This book will be useful to researchers with interests in meta-ethnography, meta-synthesis, critical interpretive synthesis and qualitative synthesis.

Claire Howell Major is Professor of the Higher Education Program at the University of Alabama, USA.

Maggi Savin-Baden is Professor of Higher Education Research at Coventry University, UK.

An Introduction to Qualitative Research Synthesis

Managing the information explosion in social science research

Claire Howell Major and
Maggi Savin-Baden

Routledge
Taylor & Francis Group

LONDON AND NEW YORK

This edition first published 2010
by Routledge
2 Park Square, Milton Park, Abingdon, Oxon, OX14 4RN

Simultaneously published in the USA and Canada
by Routledge
711 Third Avenue, New York, NY 10017

*Routledge is an imprint of the Taylor & Francis Group, an informa
business*

Transferred to Digital Printing 2010

Typeset in Galliard by
Glyph International

British Library Cataloguing in Publication Data
A catalogue record for this book is available from the British
Library

Library of Congress Cataloging-in-Publication Data
Major, Claire Howell.
    An introduction to qualitative research synthesis : managing
the information explosion in social science research / Claire
Howell Major and Maggi Savin-Baden.
        p. cm.
    Includes bibliographical references and index.
    1. Social sciences—Research—Methodology. 2. Education—
Research—Methodology. 3. Qualitative research—Methodology.
I. Savin-Baden, Maggi, 1960- II. Title.
    H62.M23583 2010
    300.72—dc22   2009024750

ISBN 10: 0-415-56285-6 (hbk)
ISBN 10: 0-415-56286-4 (pbk)

ISBN 13: 978-0-415-56285-0 (hbk)
ISBN 13: 978-0-415-56286-7 (pbk)

Contents

PART 3
Resources   113

List of figures

List of tables

List of boxes

Acknowledgements

We are most grateful for permission given to reproduce extracts from the following:

Major, C. (2010) Do virtual professors dream of electric students? College faculty experiences with online distance education. Teachers College Record, 112(8) – previously published on TCRecord.org http://www.TCRecord.org/ © Teachers College Record and reprinted here with permission.

Savin-Baden, M. and Major, C. H. (2007) Using interpretive meta-ethnography to explore the relationship between innovative approaches to learning and innovative methods of pedagogical research. *Higher Education*, 54(6): 833–52, reproduced with kind permission from Springer Science and Business Media © Springer Science + Business Media B. V. 2006.

Introduction

Claire Howell Major and Maggi Savin-Baden

We began our collaboration nearly a decade ago when we began work guest-editing a special issue of the *Journal on Excellence in College Teaching* that focused on problem-based learning. The editor had asked us to co-edit the issue as she thought we shared some common research interests. We soon realized that even though we were working in different countries, we were researching similar topics, drawing upon similar methods and participant pools, and arriving at results and conclusions that overlapped in many ways.

Maggi was working with a group of lecturers in several universities across the UK to research their experiences with problem-based learning. She relied upon narrative inquiry and semi-structured interview techniques and discovered findings related to how adopting a problem-based approach led to disjunctions that caused staff to change their teaching stances. Claire was conducting research at a single institution in the US for an ongoing study relying on narrative inquiry and semi-structured interviews. Her work led to findings about how transition to a problem-based approach changed staff knowledge of teaching and their disciplines and ultimately led to changes in teaching practices.

Comparing our work led us to many interesting conversations about the nature of knowledge and research. Over time our discussions turned to questions of how we could learn more from what we had both been doing by viewing it collectively, not only to inform our own next research steps but also to inform others about our comprehensive findings. We decided to work together to seek to uncover the knowledge that our studies, and others like them, jointly had to offer the field of problem-based learning. The question we faced was how to undertake such a task.

From the outset we acknowledged that the social science researcher's quest to extract knowledge from existing studies and their findings was nothing new. Indeed, the literature summary or literature review has long been a staple of social science research. These kinds of reviews tend to summarize, or sometimes synthesize, the arguments and ideas of others, often to argue for a new study. We knew that we could undertake such a summary or review before undertaking a new study collaboratively, but were interested in something different: a way to make meaning from existing qualitative studies viewed in aggregate. In some ways, we were seeking a parallel for qualitative research that meta-analysis has provided quantitative researchers.

Our search for a model led us initially to narrative reviews of literature, which have appeared over the past couple of decades under a variety of names, including narrative review, narrative explanatory synthesis, research synthesis, explanatory literature review and narrative literature review (see for example Cooper, 1998; Cooper and Hedges, 1994; Light and Pillemar, 1982; Pascaralla and Terenzini, 1991, 2005). Those who used these approaches most often reviewed primarily quantitative literature or did not document the kind of methodological rigour we were seeking. In contrast, we wanted a way to situate and view our studies and other qualitative studies on the same topic in relation to each other, and to discover the greater meaning implicit within the collection. Thus began our journey into learning about and using approaches to synthesizing qualitative studies.

During our investigation of various approaches to this task, we found some useful models, including qualitative meta-analysis, in which findings of qualitative studies are synthesized into a theoretical model (see for example, Bland *et al.*, 1995; Crismore, 1985; DeWitt-Brinks and Rhodes, 1992; Hager and Hasselhorn, 1998; Schreiber *et al.*, 1989). We also found meta-summary (see for example Sandelowski *et al.*, 2007) as well as grounded meta-analysis (Hossler and Scalese-Love, 1989), in which findings are aggregated through topical or thematic summaries by means of extraction and reduction of data. There were also other approaches to synthesizing qualitative evidence, such as quantitative content analysis and case survey, which tend to impose quantitative processes on qualitative data.

We found some useful approaches relying upon qualitative methods to synthesize qualitative research. Among these were the efforts in health care by the Evidence for Policy and Practice Information Centre (EPPI) in the Social Science Research Unit at the Institute of Education, University of London and the JoAnna Briggs Institute in South Australia. These provided helpful guides, but tended to be more narrative-based or aggregative than interpretive in stance; indeed, which stance is the most appropriate is a key debate in literature about synthesis of qualitative research. We learned much from this body of work as well as from some of the previously published work about synthesizing qualitative research. Perhaps most influential on our thinking was Noblit and Hare's classic text, *Meta-ethnography* (1988). We shared with these authors a belief in the importance of approaching qualitative synthesis from an interpretive stance. Trends in the nature of qualitative research during the last two decades, though, shaped our views of what processes should entail.

Ultimately we decided to devise a process for qualitative research synthesis ourselves, one that built upon the important work of others and that relied upon a critical interpretive stance that fitted our philosophical perspective. Our quest for a process ultimately bore fruit, and after presenting an early version of our work in 2003, we published our first article using the approach in 2007. In this piece we interpreted the findings of six studies about staff experiences of problem-based learning. Our original submission had caused controversy between reviewers, which required not only significant justification of our methods but also inclusion of more articles than we initially intended. Maggi later had a similar experience while working on a book chapter (Savin-Baden and Wilkie, 2004), which required justification of her selection of methods; she then completed three further studies (Sharpe and Savin-Baden, 2007; Savin-Baden *et al.*, 2007, 2008) and began conducting workshops helping other researchers learn the approach. Claire also later wrote another article using the approach (2010), with which the reviewers required extensive information about the inclusion of a small number of studies as well as about how she avoided researcher bias. She later began using the approach as an assignment in her doctoral level seminars.

After our experiences, collaborative as well as individual, we both remain committed to the approach of qualitative research synthesis for a number of reasons that we describe more fully throughout this book, particularly in Chapter 1. Among other things qualitative research synthesis:

- provides a way to deal with information explosion;
- helps researchers avoid reinventing the wheel;
- makes connections between existing studies;
- complements primary empirical studies;
- complements existing quantitative meta-analysis or -syntheses by providing a different perspective on a given phenomenon;
- provides ways to advance theory;
- helps to identify gaps and omissions in a given body of research;
- enables dialogue and debate;
- allows for development of evidence-based practice and policy;
- provides a cost-efficient approach to qualitative research.

In discussing the importance of this methodology, as well as in considering how to move the approach forward, we noted how useful we would have found it to have had a practical guide, with details and examples, of how a qualitative research synthesis could be implemented. When we first began, few guides existed. Although some useful guides have been published since (see for example Sandelowski and Barroso, 2007), we believe that by explaining our approach, we can contribute to the conversation and thus ultimately help advance the methodology. For this reason, we determined to write this book together to outline the essential elements of the process that we feel to be critical to the approach as well as to provide examples of the approach in practice.

The purpose of this book, then, is to provide a user-friendly guide to qualitative research synthesis. The intended audience for the book is broad and comprises several groups. We believe that the book will be useful to social science researchers, particularly those who are new to the approach. It provides an adaptable model for using the methodology as well as specific examples of various ways to approach it that can help novice synthesists understand and undertake the approach.

Further, for experienced synthesists, this book provides a different perspective that may be useful in considering ways to develop and refine approaches. The book also is intended to be useful to lecturers, who may wish to assign a qualitative research synthesis in lieu of a traditional research paper or research review. An assignment such as a qualitative research synthesis has numerous pedagogical advantages, including requiring students to become more critical of an existing body of research and to use higher-order thinking skills when reviewing and synthesizing literature. Indeed, lecturers may find this book to be a useful textbook and students may find it a useful supplement to research sourcebooks, as it can help guide students through the process of qualitative research synthesis. Finally, practitioners and policy makers should find this book of use. It can help them better understand the processes behind the research synthesis reports they are reading as they strive to develop evidence-based practices and policies. In short, policy makers can be better consumers of information if they have more knowledge of the processes involved in creating such research reports.

This book comprises three parts. Part 1 is our effort to provide readers with information about qualitative research synthesis so that they have the language and tools to describe and argue for the approach as well as to refute arguments against it. We provide information about the benefits and challenges of the approach in Chapter 1. In Chapter 2, we locate qualitative research synthesis within a growing tradition of review and synthesis, including those approaches we mentioned above such as qualitative meta-analysis and case synthesis. We compare its essential features and elements with other approaches.

Part 2 of this book describes the whole process of a qualitative research synthesis. In Chapter 3, we outline the process of defining the search parameters, beginning with identifying a research question suitable for a qualitative research synthesis. In this chapter, we also present approaches to searching, including electronic and hand searching. Finally, we identify ways in which studies may be evaluated for inclusion or exclusion based on quality as well as upon fit, when measured against a predetermined set of criteria. The processes of data analysis, synthesis and interpretation in qualitative research synthesis in some ways mirror those used in primary qualitative research. Several key differences exist, however, so in Chapter 4, we describe our three-part process for analysing, synthesizing and interpreting data. We provide sample templates as well as examples of how the process has been implemented.

Issues of transparency exist with any qualitative research, and in Chapter 5 we acknowledge the difficulties that are unique to qualitative research synthesis. In this chapter, we provide readers with ways of thinking about issues of plausibility, as well as specific techniques for ensuring research honesties. We outline a process that users may adapt to their own ends to ensure plausibility. In Chapter 6 we describe ways in which findings from a qualitative research synthesis may be presented, ways that allow for transparency of processes as well as products. From a description of narrative voice to examples of tables and diagrams, this chapter provides the reader with concrete information about the various forms that findings might take. In our conclusion to Parts 1 and 2, we review our rationale for writing the book, while highlighting some of the key criteria of the approach we advocate.

Finally, in Part 3 of this book, we provide the reader with resources, primarily aimed at giving the reader a sampling of the approach of qualitative research synthesis. We include executive summaries of articles that we have written using our approach. We also include the full text of an article using qualitative research synthesis, the first that we wrote (reprinted with permission), which we have annotated for this book. The purpose of including this article is to provide readers with a model, of which we have come to be critical, as only authors can be when viewing their work after significant time has elapsed. Finally, we provide readers with a bibliography of information about qualitative synthesis, more broadly, as well as a bibliography of published studies that employed it. These citations are intended to provide readers with models of qualitative research synthesis or related approaches, perhaps within their own disciplines or fields.

We hope that this book serves as a useful guide for users of qualitative research synthesis. Furthermore, we hope that it encourages conversation and debate about the approach. It is through such scholarly conversations that qualitative research synthesis can be both illuminated and advanced as an approach.

Part I

Arguing for qualitative research synthesis

Chapter 1

Making the case for qualitative research synthesis

Introduction

A number of factors have contributed to the recent drive to approach social science research differently. The morass of existing research reports, for example, has led to a kind of information overload requiring new ways of managing and making sense of them. Research, both qualitative and quantitative, is costly, and lean financial resources have made it imperative to make the most and best use of findings. A number of professional practice sectors including health care, education and social work have encountered a rise in the number and urgency of calls for accountability. Stakeholders want to know that efforts to develop new practices and programmes are effective. Calls for evidence-based practice and policy have also been on the rise, bringing current research practices into question. The underlying notion for such calls is that research should be brought closer to those who are in decision-making roles and further that research should come before an intervention or change in practice or policy (Pawson, 2002). The bottom line is that stakeholders want transparent processes, clear synthesized findings and solid recommendations for both practice and research as a result of the findings.

The convergence of such forces has sparked a debate about the purpose of social science research (see Hammersley and Foster, 1998). As a result, many have begun to view their charge differently; rather than an exercise of conducting research for research's sake, they have begun to view research as a purposeful enterprise that can help inform current professional practice. This shift in thinking has led to the drive that some feel to make the most of existing research studies, not only to manage the information and maximize the cost effectiveness, but also to show that change efforts are having an effect.

Traditional literature reviews have not been as effective at using findings as many would have hoped. Such research reviews have been criticized for a number of reasons, including their lack of precision, propensity for subjectivity and inherent biases. The task of conducting a good literature review indeed is fraught with challenges, as primary studies draw upon different methodological traditions, produce complicated findings and exist *en masse* (Cooper, 1998; Whittemore, 2005). These factors have led researchers to search for something more: a better approach for making sense of existing research studies. Qualitative research synthesis is an approach that can help accomplish that goal.

Due to the relative newness of qualitative research synthesis, as well as the questions and criticisms that synthesists may encounter, it is appropriate and important to describe the approach as well as to make a case for it. Synthesists also may find it useful to acknowledge the method's potential pitfalls, while indicating how they have avoided them. In this chapter, we provide an overview of qualitative research synthesis. We further explore what we believe are some of the most essential arguments for the method. Finally, we identify the criticisms that we have encountered most often, providing what we believe are appropriate counterpoints.

Qualitative research synthesis

At its most fundamental level, qualitative research synthesis is an approach that uses qualitative methods to analyse, synthesize and interpret the results from qualitative studies. In practice, synthesists seek to answer a specific research question through combining qualitative studies that use thick description and that are located in broadly the same tradition, in order to make sense of themes and issues across the particular data set. Qualitative research synthesis is methodologically-grounded and rigorous. It requires bringing out the qualities of meaning at a level higher from existing qualitative studies by combining them into a new whole.

In a qualitative research synthesis, synthesists undertake several specific tasks. While we describe these in more detail in Chapter 2 as well as in Part 2 of this book, here we outline the primary processes in Figure 1.1.

The process of qualitative research synthesis, while it may be described and predicted in linear terms as in Figure 1.1, is an iterative one. The search and selection phase, for example, involves instances in which the inclusion and exclusion criteria must be refined due to the articles identified, and the review of articles must be restarted. The three primary phases of analysis include 1) summarizing findings across studies and identifying which of those findings are clear and supported; 2) comparing and aggregating these findings; and 3) interpreting findings in relation to core themes that emerge across studies. Analysis requires accounting for interpretations in the original studies, which by nature demands reflexivity. The recommendations should relate to the interpretive narrative, so writing these two sections necessitates recursive activity.

Top ten arguments for using the approach

Qualitative research synthesis is valuable simply since it determines what the results of several studies, when viewed together, reveal. It is also important for the methodological contributions it makes to social science research. There also are several

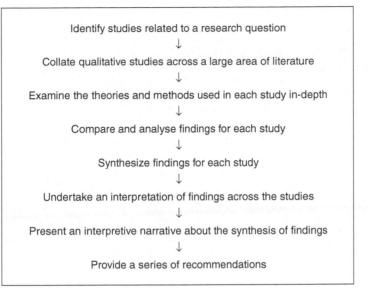

Identify studies related to a research question
↓
Collate qualitative studies across a large area of literature
↓
Examine the theories and methods used in each study in-depth
↓
Compare and analyse findings for each study
↓
Synthesize findings for each study
↓
Undertake an interpretation of findings across the studies
↓
Present an interpretive narrative about the synthesis of findings
↓
Provide a series of recommendations

Figure 1.1 Process of qualitative research synthesis.

specific arguments for using it as a research approach that goes beyond these two general attributes. Here we outline the ten we have found to be most useful.

1. Qualitative research synthesis can help contain the information explosion

Qualitative research has enjoyed a surge in popularity during the past few decades. Thousands of qualitative studies have been published in the practice professions, including nursing, medicine, business, and education in particular. This rise in the number of qualitative research studies marks an information explosion in social science research. The challenge for users is to digest and make sense of the information relevant to them. Yet mass information such as this arguably becomes unusable for many readers, researchers, practitioners and policy makers. The result can be an information overload.

Synthesizing existing information, through approaches such as qualitative research synthesis, provides a way to combine knowledge. Through qualitative research synthesis, large amounts of information are aggregated and then interpreted. The result is a research report that presents a comprehensive view of knowledge contained in multiple studies. Qualitative research synthesis then allows researchers not only to summarize an existing body of knowledge but also to discover meaning in it. Thus, the information explosion around a given topic is in some ways contained, and knowledge is rendered more comprehensible to others.

2. Qualitative research synthesis helps manage the information explosion

Related to the notion of containing the information explosion is the attending idea that it is important to manage this information as well. Due to the sheer number of studies and complications with searching, findings from original research often are lost in the data shuffle. Further, existing database management of research studies can be difficult to use, and frequently require the researcher to divine a mysterious combination of keywords, descriptors and identifiers to yield relevant research studies on a given topic. Differences in terminology in different countries (for example, staff versus faculty, as in the UK and US respectively) further complicate the search process. Hand-searching bibliographies of articles in relevant journals may help but still may not produce exhaustive results, since researchers often miss related studies.

Qualitative research synthesis offers one avenue for organizing the information that researchers have generated. It can yield research reports using studies clustered around a given topic. Synthesizing existing qualitative studies thus begins important steps in categorizing and systematizing information so that it is more readily searchable and usable. The methodology thus can provide an additional layer of filtering that can draw attention to studies that might otherwise remain obscured.

3. Qualitative research synthesis helps address the problem of knowledge fragmentation

The trend in the social sciences has been toward increased specialization. Within disciplines and fields, many new subfields have emerged. Within those subfields, many speciality areas have developed. The result is that researchers tend to identify with others in their own speciality areas and at times demonstrate little awareness of work similar to theirs that emerges from other areas. Primary research, then, often is done piecemeal, with little knowledge or acknowledgment of related work. Knowledge thus becomes fragmented and isolated. Even early proponents of qualitative methodology were worried that individual studies would become 'little islands' unto themselves, never to be linked or revisited (Glaser and Strauss, 1971: 181).

Qualitative research synthesis offers a potential solution to the problem. It is a form of qualitative research that allows for the linking of concepts across studies (Noblit and Hare, 1988). Through this approach, studies are linked based upon theories, methods and results. It requires the connecting of studies in a way that helps alleviate the issue of fragmentation of knowledge and instead seeks to build a comprehensible knowledge base. Qualitative research synthesis also helps to resolve conflicting reports of evidence (Whittemore, 2005), which helps build a research body. Finally, through qualitative research synthesis, studies can be linked across time, and in this way longitudinal study becomes more of a realistic possibility in qualitative research (Booth, 2006). Such study also helps to address the issue of fragmentation by providing a consistent chronology, which in many ways can reveal the evolution of knowledge that might otherwise appear disjointed.

4. The approach helps to identify gaps and omissions in a given body of research or within a single article

Researchers often seek to develop a 'line' of research. The notion is that moving forward incrementally and in a single direction is the best way to advance knowledge. However, as different researchers move along different lines, gaps between the lines begin to occur. Qualitative research synthesis is one way to start to view individual lines of research as connected lines, and thus to begin to develop a web of knowledge. This approach also can make the gaps between the lines more apparent, and thus can illustrate the kinds of studies that are needed to bridge those gaps.

In addition, researchers can tend to short-hand methodology sections, assuming that readers understand a given context or even research design, which may or may not be the case, so methodological gaps can be apparent within a given study. One of the primary features of qualitative research synthesis is that it requires synthesists to conduct a critical appraisal of each study around a given topic. The appraisal involves an evaluation of 'fit' based upon both applicability and quality. As synthesists makes decisions about inclusion and exclusion of studies, mistakes or omissions in existing articles become much clearer. Synthesists then can provide critical interpretations of strengths and limitations not only of individual studies but also of the aggregated view of them, thereby changing and potentially advancing the field.

5. Qualitative research synthesis provides a different perspective on questions addressed through quantitative approaches

Many meta-analytic studies have been conducted over the past decades that have extended knowledge in several ways. Quantitative researchers who have conducted these studies have done so under the guiding assumption that there is a body of knowledge that has been collected and amassed that can inform thinking collectively. These studies necessarily are directed by what is available in the literature. The questions meta-analytic researchers tend to ask then generally are derivative of the questions asked by the primary researchers.

Like meta-analytic researchers, synthesists generally derive their questions from those that exist in the literature. By examining different questions and combining different sets of evidence, synthesists can help provide even greater illumination of a topic, which may complement what quantitative meta-analysis has revealed. Thus, 'is anxiety management an effective way of replacing alcohol as a coping strategy in clients with dependency problems?' might best be addressed through a systematic review of quantitative evidence. However, 'how may practitioners help clients deal with the effects of sudden and traumatic disability on their occupational behaviour?' could be answered by reviewing qualitative studies of the experiences of disabled people as they deal with their changing life circumstances, thus investigating a topic through a different lens. As another example, if a quantitative meta-analysis investigated the question of whether students learn as effectively in an online environment as they do in a face-to-face situation, the researcher might be able to answer affirmatively or negatively, based upon what existing studies show. A qualitative research synthesis would begin with a different question, such as how students learn in an online environment. The findings of such a synthesis would involve a range of information such as approaches to learning, engagement with others and study skills. Thus the two approaches taken together could provide powerful information to staff wishing to operate online (or arguing against it) as well as to policy makers issuing guidelines for online learning.

6. Qualitative research synthesis provides ways to advance theory

As we have noted above, there are many disadvantages linked to the fact that primary qualitative research is done by way of disconnected studies that do not allow for the accumulation of knowledge. One of the primary disadvantages is that new theories rarely are developed or tested. It is difficult to drive the development of a discipline or field without the advancement of the theoretical base.

Qualitative research synthesis requires reflection and theorizing by design. In this way, it can allow researchers to consider findings from a philosophical and theoretical perspective that allows for development of the discipline (Paterson et al., 2001; Ritzer, 1992). Due to this unique opportunity, synthesis can add to theory building in a way that no single study could alone. Indeed, theory building is one of the most important contributions of qualitative synthesis (Paterson et al., 2001). Thus the method can help fulfil the obligation to develop theory to which many researchers aspire.

7. Qualitative research synthesis can spark dialogue and debate

Often findings from individual qualitative studies are not discussed or challenged. Rarely do findings invite interdisciplinary or even disciplinary conversations. Qualitative research synthesis may begin dialogues or debates that drive the development of a discipline (Bondas and Hall, 2007). It may accomplish this end as synthesists put information into a form that is more accessible to others, who then can consider it for its contribution. Furthermore, in making recommendations for future research and practice, synthesists may stimulate discussion not only of the issues and the findings, but also of whether and how they should be applied.

8. Qualitative research synthesis can add a depth dimension to qualitative studies

Qualitative research has been valued because of its ability to provide depth of information about a particular phenomenon. The research report is a rich, thick description of a snapshot in time and place. Qualitative studies allow the reader a glimpse of the lived experience of a small group of study participants. This advantage can also be a challenge, as providing depth often is done at the exclusion of providing breadth of examination.

Synthesis research does not take the place of original empirical studies, but rather complements them (Campbell *et al.*, 2003; Ritzer, 1992; Zhao, 1991). One of the ways that it accomplishes this end is by pursuing both depth and breadth simultaneously. Qualitative research synthesis can provide an overarching and comprehensive glimpse of what the in-depth individual qualitative snapshots reveal. Through retaining some of the dense description of the original data, the broader picture provides some detail that conveys the experiences of the original participants.

9. The approach can allow for development of evidence-based practice and policy

The evidence-based policy movement originated as evidence-based *medicine* and so began from a quantitative and 'hard science' perspective. The established hierarchy of evidence very clearly has systematic reviews and randomized control trials (RCTs) at its head (Taylor, 2000). However, this focus on RCTs as 'best' evidence has not sat comfortably with many non-medical evidence-based practitioners (Dublouloz *et al.*, 1999; Taylor, 1997; Tickle-Degnen, 1999). The notion of 'best' evidence has been debated within evidence-based practice (for example evidence-based health archives, 1998). The place of the RCT as the 'gold standard' has been contested and reviewed. Evidence-based practitioners (see for example Sackett and Wennberg, 1997) have begun to acknowledge that RCTs cannot answer every question about interventions and practices. Thus evidence may be seen not only as valid and reliable statistical data, but also as integrated forms of data and a whole host of qualitative evidence, the kind of information that a qualitative research synthesis readily provides.

Further, qualitative research synthesis can provide answers from a range of research, which most users of research (i.e. practitioners and policy makers) are more comfortable in relying on, in preference to results from only one individual study (Gough, 2007). Thus those working in policy positions may be more likely to use research to inform policy development. Those working in granting agencies may be more able to use findings to make funding decisions. Finally, those in practical roles within organizations may be able to make data-informed front-line decisions.

10. Qualitative research synthesis is a cost-efficient approach

In conducting qualitative research today several elements are essential. The process requires time from a researcher or a research team. It also requires equipment for data collection such as cameras, tape recorders and video recorders as well as equipment for data storage. Qualitative research requires time and equipment for transcription as well as time for coding, and often special equipment. Due to these factors, qualitative research is expensive and is becoming more so as the cost of researcher time increases and the addition of advanced technology increases equipment costs.

Qualitative research synthesis can help to defray costs associated with research. It accomplishes this end by optimizing findings from individual studies (Thorne, 1994). In particular, while some factors such as researcher costs remain constant, other costs such as those associated with time for data collection, collection equipment, and even transcription, may be greatly reduced if not eliminated.

Top ten criticisms of the approach, point and counterpoint

While the advantages of qualitative research synthesis seem clear, the approach is not without criticism. Many researchers, though, have argued for the potential of synthesis methods and have suggested ways to improve the processes (see for example Doyle, 2003; Egger et al., 1997; Rantala and Wellstrom, 2001; Savin-Baden and Major, 2007; Shkedi, 2005; Weed, 2006). In this section we describe the ten criticisms we have encountered most often and offer advice for countering them.

1. Qualitative research synthesis is really just a literature review

Point: It is tempting to suggest that a qualitative research synthesis is in essence a literature review. It does, after all, involve selection of a topic for research, a search for literature, an evaluation of the data and finally the presentation of information contained in existing literature into a logical whole. Qualitative research synthesis has even been categorized as a type of literature review by many who use it or similar approaches (see for example Pope et al., 2007).

Counterpoint: We believe that the 'uses' or 'treatment' of research in social sciences fall along a continuum of criticality, from least to most critical in stance, which we describe and illustrate more fully in Chapter 2. Literature reviews tend to involve an attempt to produce a description or demonstration of a state of knowledge about a given topic. Analysis marks another movement along the continuum, with meta-analysis being an example. If one wishes to argue that meta-analysis is a literature review, then one could similarly make that claim for qualitative research synthesis. But we believe that both of these approaches involve more than a 'review'. Both also involve searching for studies to answer a specific question as well as breaking down component findings and analysing the parts. Further, they both involve presenting a synthesis of some sort, although meta-analysis is a synthesis from a positivist perspective (looking at individual parts as they fit into a whole), while qualitative research synthesis is done from an interpretivist perspective, which requires looking at the whole created by the individual parts. Further, qualitative research synthesis involves reinterpretation of data. In short, findings from qualitative studies are treated as data, which undergo analysis, synthesis and interpretation. In the words of Noblit and Hare, originators of the method, 'it is much more than what we generally mean by a literature review' (1988: 9).

2. Synthesists are restricted by what is already available in the literature

Point: Some authors argue that conducting a synthesis can be confining. The synthesist's creativity arguably is restricted to what is available in published form (whether through peer reviewed publication or 'grey' literature). In particular, synthesists are limited in that they can only study topics that other researchers have investigated. Further, synthesists are limited to specific questions that have already been investigated and which have appeared in published form. Finally, synthesists are constrained by the information that is provided in the published studies, in particular to data that has been presented in the original studies.

Counterpoint: Due to the wide variety of qualitative studies to date, synthesists have a range of original studies and thus topics at their disposal. Many critical questions worthy of investigation have already been undertaken by researchers, and thus a wealth of information exists. Many questions have been asked and it is important to make meaning of those before moving on. Research should be a building process; otherwise, we are only ever laying the foundation, without setting any cornerstones or building the structure. Furthermore, we believe that the questions that a synthesist asks can extend beyond the questions that have been asked in the literature. We assert that developing a question can be a type of synthesis, as synthesists scan the literature for questions that have been asked and aggregate them into a comprehensive or overarching question. So the research question for a synthesis then ultimately is a 'meta-question'.

Presentation of data can be a limiting factor, particularly if the authors of the primary articles provided scanty descriptions from original text. Synthesists can set boundaries in study selection criteria (see Chapter 3) to exclude studies that do not present data. Beyond the original data presented, many argue that other aspects of the article, such as the title and discussion, also are data (see Noblit and Hare (1988) for example).

3. There is too much variety among qualitative methods for synthesis to be meaningful

Point: Another criticism of qualitative research synthesis is that qualitative research is still in the process of developing a firm methodology. Many different approaches exist and many qualitative researchers use terms imprecisely. Many researchers are guilty of inadequately describing their methodology sections in their publications, and thus synthesists may not have adequate information to assess the viability of the design nor may they truly understand what the research design is, since some researchers have different interpretations of what the various qualitative research designs entail. It is difficult, then, to select studies in which methods are exact, yet taking studies together tends to ignore methodological difference. Synthesists, it may be argued further, have not been involved in the research design phase and thus have not had any control over the methodology or methods.

Counterpoint: In quantitative meta-analysis studies often are selected because of standardized methods of data collection and analysis. Arguing for such precision and exactness is overlaying positivist frames on interpretive inquiry, which we believe should be avoided. Yet even within this positivist framework, some scholars (see for example Noblit and Hare, 1988) have argued that meta-studies need to be broad enough in design to allow for inclusion of evidence collected by various approaches. Few synthesists have argued that research methods must be exact, but rather congruent and consistent. In qualitative syntheses, it is argued that studies should be selected based on *similar* designs. Data collected using interview methods, whether for a basic or generic qualitative design or a grounded theory study or something else, may still be evaluated on the information they provide from the first-hand perspective of the participant. Further, some have argued (see for example Bondas and Hall, 2007) that it is the findings that are more important than the method of data collection, which may have more surface similarity than actual similarity.

It is true that synthesists have not been involved in the design and thus have had no say in it. They do however have a say in which studies will be included or excluded from the synthesis. Synthesists may elect to tightly control what articles will be included, according to criteria they find acceptable, or they may choose to loosely control the selection to be more inclusive of articles with different but congruent research approaches. It is true that synthesists may not have all of the information necessary for analysis and interpretation, but again, they may choose to exclude those studies without sufficient information on the grounds that they are fatally flawed. Alternatively, through the process of member checking, authors of the primary studies can be questioned in order to determine missing information (see Chapter 5) Finally, it is true that researchers can at times interpret various qualitative traditions differently from others, but if they have done an adequate job of describing the research process, then terminology does not have to be the deciding factor; rather, synthesists can exclude or include studies based upon the actual approach followed instead of having to rely solely upon what the original researcher called the approach.

4. The researcher lacks access to primary data

Point: It has been suggested that it is a challenge that researchers do not have access to primary data (Heaton, 2004; Thorne, 1994, 1998). Lacking such access makes reanalysis of inherited data (i.e. secondary analysis) impossible. Thus, qualitative research synthesis is not primary research, nor is it precisely secondary research.

Counterpoint: While it is true that synthesists do not have access to primary data, some do not see this as a disadvantage, and instead believe it actually may be an advantage of the approach. If synthesists were to use original transcripts, as is done in secondary analysis, then they would not have the same contextual clues that the original researcher had when interpreting the data. They would not have seen facial expressions or environmental expressions of culture or other issues. Thus researchers 'conducting the re-analysis might understand the data differently from its collector' (Rantala and Wellstrom, 2001: 88). Conducting reanalysis then could lead to conflicting reports or to errors in interpretation. Since qualitative research synthesis does not involve the review of full sets of raw data, however, but rather focuses on the interpretations of that data, the interpretations of the original researcher, who did have these clues, may be retained. Thus, interpretations in qualitative research synthesis have the potential to convey meaning nested within context, whereas raw data could not (Doyle, 2003; Weed, 2006).

5. Context is stripped

Point: Some may argue that in synthesis, research studies are considered together and thus context, critical to the qualitative tradition, is stripped away. Rich, thick description is a part of the qualitative tradition, yet the treatment of any given article through the process of synthesis can lead to thinned descriptions. This stripping and thinning, it is argued, undermines the purpose of qualitative research.

Counterpoint: There are numerous ways for a synthesist to provide information about the context of the original studies, to the extent that such information is available. Among the ways is through providing evidence of common research goals and topics in the original studies. Another is to provide evidence of common research questions and research designs used to conduct the original investigations. Another still is taking care to provide sufficient contextual information about the research site and setting (Savin-Baden and Major, 2007). In these ways, synthesists may retain and articulate important context.

6. Researcher bias may be an issue

Point: Just as with any qualitative research project, issues of researcher bias may call the approach into question. In particular, some may question whether the researcher has too vested an interest in the topic to be truly objective. The researcher not only devises the question, but also selects the study sample and conducts the interpretation. Bias coupled with control could lead to inaccurate interpretations.

Counterpoint: The quest for objectivity is one that is not usually found by either quantitative or qualitative researchers, no matter how hard they strive for it. The quest itself, however, originates from the positivist paradigm, which as we noted above, we believe is an inappropriate paradigm under which to construct or evaluate qualitative processes. In naturalistic or interpretive inquiry the researcher generally strives for working against bias, and for transparency and plausibility. A rigorous reporting and reflection system can help the researcher achieve these attributes (Savin-Baden and Major, 2007; Major, 2010).

7. Validity is not established in qualitative research synthesis

Point: One point some make against qualitative research synthesis is that including several studies that may have congruent, but not precisely the same, research question is not valid. Furthermore, having congruent, but not precisely the same, research designs may mean that the study does not measure what it says that it measures. Such imprecision may mean that the study is not rigorous, and thus is not believable.

Counterpoint: Validity is not something for which qualitative researchers generally strive. They tend to seek for 'trustworthiness', 'credibility', 'honesties', or other approaches that assert that truth is a fragile concept, while acknowledging that some efforts must be taken to assure the reader that the account can be relied upon. In qualitative research synthesis by design, the research report is grounded in information gleaned from a number of methods from a variety of studies conducted across time and place. Furthermore, synthesists can and should seek to ensure their interpretations are plausible by employing a range of approaches which we describe further in Chapter 6.

8. Too few studies are included in qualitative research syntheses to allow for generalizabilty and transferability

Point: Some reviewers that we have encountered have suggested that too few studies and thus too few participants are included in qualitative research synthesis projects to make the results meaningful in other settings. They also argue that the findings cannot be transferred to other situations. In short, the synthesis is not generalizable to other situations.

Counterpoint: Qualitative research synthesis provides a mechanism for capitalizing on the studies available. There are generally far more participants included in a qualitative synthesis than in a primary qualitative study. For example, if a qualitative research synthesis article has included six studies that each has ten participants, then the synthesis has 60 participants for inclusion as well as at least six researchers. Sixty six participants is a generally high number for a qualitative study, so arguing that it is an insufficient number seems fundamentally to undervalue qualitative research processes.

Furthermore, qualitative studies rarely seek to be generalizable to a larger population. Arguing for generalizability also seems to be hostile to a qualitative perspective. Finally, results from qualitative studies may or may not be transferable to other situations. It is up to the researcher to provide sufficient information about the research process so that others, whether researchers, practitioners or policy makers, can gauge transferability. We argue that methods may be more readily transferable to other settings than results, although it is critical to provide sufficient methodological detail to determine whether methods or results have applicability elsewhere.

9. Qualitative research synthesis can lead to the devaluation of qualitative work

Point: Qualitative researchers undertake their craft for a variety of reasons, most often selecting their methodology based upon deeply held beliefs and philosophical perspectives. They spend hours in the field and in coding data. Many have worked diligently to ensure the development and rigour of the research approach. If qualitative research synthesis is undertaken with an agenda to criticize and point out weaknesses in what already has been done, it not only undervalues but also devalues important headway that has been made.

Counterpoint: Qualitative research synthesis must be undertaken with care. Synthesists must ensure that they point out not only the challenges with a given body of work but also the important contributions that individual studies have made (Paterson et al, 2001). Qualitative synthesis must also be undertaken with the same standards of rigour to which primary research studies have adhered. In this way, they can avoid undermining primary qualitative research studies but also seek important methodological advances that may have application in primary research.

10. Qualitative research synthesis uses participants and researchers' work without their permission

Point: Qualitative research synthesists have not gone through traditional paths for gaining study approval, such as Institutional Research Board Review. They have not asked participants whether they are willing to participate in the synthesis, and thus they may marginalize the voices of participants. Furthermore, most frequently they have not sought author approval to use their studies in the synthesis.

Counterpoint: Synthesists rely upon published data. As such, it is available to readers and researchers for a variety of purposes, such as improving policy, teaching knowledge and informing current and future research. By publishing the work, the author has consented to its dissemination and use. Further, researchers of the original studies have undergone ethical clearance, which ensures that participants' rights are being respected. It is the synthesists' responsibility to retain the integrity of the original study and to present a coherent narrative that is respectful to participants. It is our hope that in Part 2 we have provided sound guidance on how to do that.

Conclusion

In this chapter, we provided an overview of qualitative research synthesis, highlighting the processes, benefits, and potential pitfalls of the methodology. Beyond this general introduction to the approach, however, we believe that to engage with it, it is important to understand how it differs from other approaches that fall within the growing tradition of research synthesis. For this reason, in Chapter 2 we further explicate the essential features of qualitative research synthesis in order to compare it with other approaches.

Chapter 2

Comparing qualitative research synthesis with other approaches

Introduction

The question of what can, and should, be done with existing literature has confounded generations of scholars. The resulting efforts to make use of research findings specifically, however, have led to the emergence of a range of approaches that have drawn from ever increasing levels of specialization, criticality and interpretation. These approaches over time have grown more complex and refined in both application and technique. Qualitative research synthesis, which relies upon sophisticated interpretivist methods for implementation, is one approach that has developed from these efforts. In this chapter, we not only identify where qualitative research synthesis falls within the traditions of literature use but also outline its essential features and elements, thus allowing its comparison to other approaches. Finally, we discuss the increasing use of qualitative research synthesis in several professional practice fields.

Uses of literature: A framework for understanding

Several scholars have attempted to categorize and classify various types of literature reviews and have developed a number of interesting schemes for doing so. Pope *et al.* (2007) for example, argue that there are two generations of literature reviews. The first generation involves a more simplistic view of literature in which existing research is simply reported and described. The second generation involves more direct analysis of the literature, by way of either quantitative or qualitative methods of analysis.

We believe that assessments such as Pope *et al.*'s are useful and that they help us begin to understand the various approaches to literature and research findings. Our view differs from theirs somewhat, however, in that rather than two distinct, even if overlapping, generations of literature reviews, we believe that 'use' of research can more accurately be described as falling along a continuum of criticality. By 'use' we mean the general definition as in 'to employ for some purpose or service'. We make 'use' of research when we take findings and turn them into a particular form. The continuum we envision involves various phases of transitions of one form of research use into another. Therefore, any given phase on the scale cannot be achieved without meeting the standards of the one that preceded it. By criticality, we mean the behaviour of those who are engaged in the various phases on the scale and the complex cognitive functions required to construct an explanation of data that they must perform at each phase. Thus we argue that it is possible to locate use of research literature on a continuum as follows:

1	2	3	4	5	6
Research as information	Research as justification	Research as demonstration	Research as account	Research as part of whole	Research as representation

Figure 2.1 Forms of literature use, along a continuum.

As we have illustrated, all of these forms represent 'use' of literature. We further believe that there are various 'levels' of use and that qualitative research synthesis falls within one set of these levels. In order to illustrate how we view the positioning of qualitative research synthesis within these various levels and forms of use, we offer Figure 2.2.

Finally, we believe that these various uses of literature correspond with overt research forms, as we will describe in the next few sections. In these sections, we use the levels to provide the overarching organizational structure and interpose the forms of use as subsections.

Synopses of findings

While all of the approaches involve an accounting or summing up of findings, we see two approaches to literature uses as falling solely within this level: Forms 1 and 2.

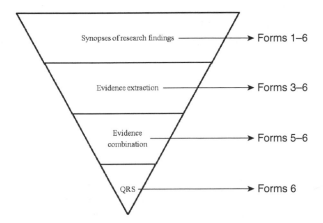

Figure 2.2 The position of qualitative research synthesis, among levels of use.

Forms 1 and 2 Research as information and justification: the literature review or summary

Research as 'information' or research as 'justification' both involve 'reviews' that often are incorporated into other works. Those who use research as 'information', we believe, go about the basic function of simply presenting, many times in a case by case documentation, the body of work around a given subject area. Their intent often is to provide a basic introduction or background to a broad topical area. We find that students often use this approach, whether intentionally or unintentionally; as they strive to 'review' literature, they often do so in a text by text approach, summarizing the contents of each work. Another example of the information approach is the annotated bibliography. Those who use research as 'justification' tend to present it in order to set the stage for the proposed study, often casting the 'review' as an argument that the study should be done, accomplished by demonstrating where gaps exist. This form often manifests in the traditional social science 'literature review' in a research report.

Evidence extraction

The remaining four Forms (3–6), which all require evidence extraction, generally appear as stand-alone studies. We believe that the first two of these, research as demonstration and research as account, involve approaches that primarily rely upon extracting information from findings and recounting it and thus are positioned solely at this level.

Form 3 Research as demonstration: the research review

The first of the forms of evidence extraction, literature as 'demonstration,' involves an accounting of research reports around a given phenomenon to document what the research has shown. These often are cast as 'narrative reviews' of research. This form of use is similar to that of a traditional research report in that it gathers information around a broad topic and summarizes the findings. These reviews differ from traditional literature reviews in that they require analysis; however, the types of analysis generally is not specified, although at times there is a general mention of 'weight of evidence' criteria, in the sense that if a preponderance of evidence demonstrates a finding, it is considered credible.

Form 4 Research as account: the research analysis

Using literature as an 'account' involves seeing research as a collection of various elements or components that may be viewed independently in an effort to either support or refute various assertions. They focus on a narrow question and often involve an examination of literature with similar research questions using analytic techniques to organize information into common sub-elements.

These forms were developed initially as methods when findings of more traditional or narrative reviews were called into question. Meta-analysis is a primary example of this type of 'review', and the originator of this approach (Glass, 1976) challenged the findings of a traditional review by applying statistical techniques and examining effect size.

Evidence combination

Due to the many demands that we outlined in Chapter 1, approaches to combining evidence have become something of a cottage industry over these past few decades. A range of approaches for undertaking, managing and making sense of existing studies have come to the fore as researchers have struggled to find effective ways to accomplish the task. What these approaches share is a core mission to develop systematic and rigorous methods for combining evidence (Whittemore, 2005). We believe that two forms of use fall within the level of evidence combination: research as part of whole and research as representation.

Form 5 Research as part of whole: the research synthesis

While reviews and analyses break down the findings into parts and present them in a disaggregated fashion, synthesis involves aggregating information into a new and unified whole. One of these approaches, research as 'part of whole' involves looking at literature from the perspective that individual parts can be viewed collectively to understand a larger picture. Syntheses, like analyses, focus on a narrow question. They may be seen as a combination and aggregation of previous research with similar questions using a rigorous and methodologically grounded approach. It is important to note that syntheses, like reviews and analyses before them, began with syntheses of quantitative evidence, often in the medical profession and often relying upon meta-analysis as the technique of data analysis. An example of this type of synthesis is the systematic review, an approach which is supported by multiple organizations including the Cochrane Collaborative, the Campbell Collaboration, EPPI-Center, and the Centre for Reviews and Dissemination.

Many scholars, however, began to believe it important to include qualitative evidence in systematic review as well. The approaches that have emerged as a result most often involve reducing data from qualitative or mixed method studies to quantifiable units so that they may be analysed with quantitative approaches, although some have adopted meta-ethnographic approaches. Such analysis ranges great degrees in analytical complexity.

The most common approaches to combining qualitative or qualitative and quantitative findings are quantitative content analysis, quantitative case survey, 'qualitative' comparative analysis, realist synthesis and narrative synthesis from systematic review. Quantitative content analysis basically involves reviewing text of studies and translating them into countable parts. Quantitative case survey involves reviewing multiple case studies and translating findings into variables that can be analysed statistically. Qualitative comparative analysis involves translating qualitative studies into variables that can be analysed to determine which are required to produce a certain outcome. Realist synthesis involves reviewing qualitative or quantitative evidence and using either quantitative or qualitative methods for analysis, depending upon the purpose and needs of the study. Narrative synthesis involves systematic review of research that is either qualitative or quantitative and using a narrative approach for synthesizing them. We outline the essential elements of these main forms in Table 2.1.

What these approaches share is an emphasis on reducing large amounts of data into smaller more manageable components that often can be counted in some way. The advantage of these approaches is that they are inexpensive, compact approaches to managing large amounts of data in ways that frequently can show relationships among variables. The primary disadvantages include the fact that they are reductionist in approach and thus can undermine the most essential features of qualitative research: context and interpretation. Furthermore, they have varying levels of transparency and do not always control or discuss the potential of bias.

Form 6 Research as representation: Qualitative synthesis

Over time scholar-synthesists began to feel a sense of unease with approaches that imposed quantitative frameworks on qualitative research. Many soon began to recognize the value of qualitative literature, ceding the point that qualitative research findings have something different to offer knowledge than quantitative studies. This acknowledgment prompted the development of more qualitative, critical and interpretive approaches (which we believe can exist simultaneously) to combining evidence from qualitative studies. A few varieties of such approaches have emerged, most of which are derived from Noblit and Hare's classic work, *Meta-ethnography*. Noblit and Hare (1988: 9) state that their approach 'enables a rigorous procedure for deriving substantive interpretations about any set of ethnographic or interpretive studies. ... A meta-ethnography can be considered a complete study in itself. [Meta-ethnography] compares and analyzes texts, creating new interpretations in the process'.

Noblit and Hare's work, it may be argued, has sparked a revolution in synthesis that involves qualitative approaches to synthesizing qualitative evidence. A qualitative synthesis, then, uses qualitative methods to synthesize existing qualitative studies to construct greater meaning through an interpretive process. It involves focusing on a narrow research question, as well as an interpretation of previous research with similar questions while using a rigorous and methodologically grounded approach for analysis that is filtered through an interpretive lens. The approach requires translation which in turn drives meaning.

What's in a name? Qualitative research synthesis

While we started our work together with this research approach on a 'meta-ethnographic study,' and are still closest to the methodology created by

Table 2.1 Approaches to combining evidence

Method	Quantitative content analysis	Quantitative case survey	'Qualitative' comparative analysis	Realist synthesis	Systematic review with narrative synthesis
Description and process	A systematic technique for reviewing text of articles, highlighting and generalizing dominant findings and counting them.	A systematic technique for reviewing findings of multiple cases.	A systematic technique for summarizing and comparing findings from case studies, for the absence or presence of variables.	A systematic process involving an eclectic, iterative approach to synthesis.	A systematic technique for summarizing the results of studies and presenting a narrative synthesis of results.
Purpose/aim	To identify findings and make generalizations about them; to present a quantitative picture from a range of evidence.	To aggregate findings; to make statistical comparisons of multiple variables across studies. To generalize to larger populations.	To identify the necessary conditions required to produce an outcome.	To test theories or mechanisms.	To summarize and explain findings of multiple studies
Forms of evidence included	Quantitative and qualitative findings (can also be used with visual and audio-visual materials)	Qualitative or mixed method case studies	Case studies	A wide range, including research findings (qualitative and quantitative), reports, grey literature.	Qualitative and quantitative research findings

Exclusion criteria	Not specified	Usually little. If done, based upon internal validity (bias) or external validity (generalizability)	All cases related to a phenomenon are considered; cases are eliminated if only one explanatory variable produces the outcome (labelled logically irrelevant)	Test relevance (do the findings address theory); Test rigour (do the findings support conclusions)	Predetermined 'objective' exclusion criteria, often based upon study relevance or quality.
Method of data collection	Studies reviewed by way of questionnaire	Studies reviewed with structured questionnaire	Studies reviewed for a similar set of variables	Theories extracted from literature; findings extracted.	Findings of studies extracted
Intends to measure	Frequencies	Outcome relationship to explanatory variables	Variables associated with a particular outcome	What works under which circumstance	Outcomes of intervention
Treatment	Cases are selected and reviewed. Variables are extracted. Coding with explicit rules; exclusive and exhaustive categories identified in advance	Cases are selected and reviewed. Variables are extracted and aggregated. Patterns are sought across studies. Coding schemes for converting qualitative cases into quantifiable variables.	Cases are selected and reviewed. Coding using binary according to whether variable is present.	Literature is searched for relevant theories. Theories are listed, grouped and developed into an evaluative framework to be populated with evidence. Research studies are sought, appraised and findings are extracted. Findings are then synthesized, and conclusions drawn.	Studies are located, selected and critically appraised. They are reviewed for data. Data is analysed. Results are interpreted.

Continued

Table 2.1 Cont'd

Method	Quantitative content analysis	Quantitative case survey	'Qualitative' comparative analysis	Realist synthesis	Systematic review with narrative synthesis
Analysis	Descriptive statistics	Statistical analysis (could involve meta-analysis)	Summary and comparison by simple algorithms based on Boolean logic.	Evaluative document developed, based upon theories; analysis may be quantitative or qualitative or both, selected depending upon the hypothesis to be tested.	Statistical analysis, such as a meta-analysis, used in analysis; increasingly studies are summarized using qualitative approaches (sometimes termed a qualitative systematic review)
Researcher/s role/s	Multiple assessors, inter-rater agreement	Multiple assessors, inter-rater agreement	Not specified	Not specified	Not specified
Presentation	Tables	Cross case matrices or summary tables	Tables	Narrative	Narrative

Noblit and Hare, over time, we settled upon the term 'qualitative research synthesis' for a number of reasons. First, since quantitative meta-analysis is a well established term and well understood approach, we, in some ways, were seeking a term that was as apt for the process we advocate as meta-analysis is for its process. We worked for a while with the term qualitative meta-synthesis because of the similar structure to quantitative meta-analysis but ultimately determined that those who tend to use meta-synthesis generally (although not always) are referring to a more aggregative than interpretive approach, and thus it was not the most apt. Further, we were not looking for a direct parallel to quantitative meta-analysis, for as we describe in this chapter, we do not see them as parallel approaches. The qualitative research synthesis, however, is related to 'quantitative meta-analysis' in this important way: in quantitative meta-analysis, quantitative methods are applied to understanding quantitative findings. Similarly, in qualitative research synthesis, qualitative methods are applied to interpreting qualitative findings. So both approaches have the requirement of congruence between methods of synthesis and the primary study forms. We believe this consistency makes them more easily comprehensible to potential users.

Second, we believe that the term qualitative research synthesis best expresses the process. The component parts of the term are important and reveal the fitness of expression. The term 'qualitative' stresses the distinctions based on qualities, rather than quantities. The term synthesis means that elements of separate materials are combined into a single or unified identity. We recognize that by adding the central term 'research,' the phrase may be read in two ways, depending which of the other terms one reads the word 'research' as aligned with. Consider the difference between 'qualitative research' synthesis and qualitative 'research synthesis'. When we employ the phrase, we mean both readings: a qualitative synthesis of qualitative research.

Third, the term is precise enough to demarcate it from other approaches with similar monikers. As we indicate in Table 2.1, the many approaches to reviewing, analysing, and synthesizing qualitative research have been called a variety of names, sometimes for seemingly the same processes. Meta-ethnography, meta-synthesis, qualitative meta-synthesis, among others have all been used to describe seemingly similar processes. All of these approaches share a common goal of using qualitative approaches to synthesizing qualitative research, and thus have much to offer each other. The term 'qualitative research synthesis,' which seems the most inclusive of all of these concepts, then, is, we believe, the most effective construction.

Fourth, the term qualitative research synthesis does not add to the research jargon. While we were tempted to experiment with the term in an effort to capture the interpretive nature of the process we expose, in the end, we simply did not want to further complicate the literature. Qualitative research synthesis is gaining ground as the most frequently used moniker for the approach (Suri and Clarke, 2009) and thus the best one to select for our purposes.

Fifth, while our approach resembles the classic work of Noblit and Hare (1988), we do not believe that the term meta-ethnography currently is the most appropriate for several reasons. Today the term meta-ethnography seems a bit unfriendly and thus it has the propensity to deter some researchers who might otherwise engage with it, which could hinder advancement of the approach. Further, while the term meta-ethnography indeed was provocative 20 years ago when Noblit and Hare first used it, the variety of approaches to qualitative research that have developed during the last two decades limits its applicability. For this reason, we think the term is no longer the most precise expression of what most synthesis researchers do. The studies most frequently used in qualitative synthesis are not ethnographies, but rather are other forms of qualitative approaches; while Noblit and Hare did try to incorporate the broader meaning into their definition of meta-ethnography, the fact is that many qualitative researchers still argue about the lack of precision of the term.

In our own work, we tend toward qualitative research synthesis for philosophical reasons. This approach tends to be the most inclusive and interpretive in nature. It tends to examine a small enough data set so that original interpretations may be retained. It allows the researcher greater ability for reflection and criticality. Thus the term qualitative research synthesis best fits our needs.

Key differences between qualitative research synthesis and critical interpretive synthesis

Approaches based upon meta-ethnographic methods appear in two main forms: qualitative research synthesis and critical interpretive review. The different elements of these approaches may be seen in Table 2.2.

The common elements of these approaches, then, involve translating studies into each other and interpreting the results.

We note that the approach we argue for on its face value is similar to critical interpretive synthesis (see Dixon-Woods *et al.*, 2007), alternately termed simply 'meta-synthesis' (see Bair and Haworth, 2005), which while it tends to adopt qualitative research synthesis, or meta-ethnographic approaches, applies them to both quantitative and qualitative studies and generally draws upon a much larger sample size than qualitative research synthesis. We note that much important work has been done by those who have undertaken such approaches. We believe, however, that despite surface similarities, qualitative research synthesis and critical interpretive synthesis are fundamentally different approaches, although they can inform each other. While qualitative research synthesis approaches the question with an in-depth approach to analysis, synthesis and interpretation, modified approaches seek more breadth than depth. As a result of this, the processes, though requiring similar steps, actually require quite different cognitive functions.

As a result of these differences, we note the processes that we outline in Part 2 of this book are based upon our experiences with synthesizing qualitative studies only. We hope that synthesists who wish to review both qualitative and quantitative

Table 2.2 Qualitative approaches to combining qualitative evidence

Method	Meta-ethnography/qualitative research synthesis	Critical interpretive synthesis/meta-synthesis
Description and process	Qualitative research synthesis involves reinterpretation and translation of concepts in one student into another. It combines primary studies into a new whole.	Meta-ethnographic approach applied, but included are quantitative studies, particularly the discussion and conclusion sections
Purpose/aim	To develop a conceptual translation, a reinterpretation of data or development of a new theory	To allow for a meta-ethnographic approach to synthesizing both qualitative and quantitative studies
Forms of evidence included	Qualitative studies only	Quantitative and qualitative studies
Exclusion criteria	Predetermined by the researcher, generally based upon topic, research question, research methodology and clear findings.	Predetermined by the researcher
Method of data collection	Searching for studies until saturation is reached	Comprehensive sampling
Intends to measure	A comprehensive picture of findings from individual studies	A comprehensive picture of findings from individual studies
Treatment	Key concepts and themes are extracted from findings, and frequently from author discussions, conclusions, title, etc.	Key concepts and themes are extracted from findings of qualitative studies and discussion sections of quantitative studies.
Analysis	Standard qualitative techniques such as coding and constant comparison	Standard qualitative techniques such as coding and constant comparison
Researcher(s) role(s)	Assuming an interpretive stance	Assuming an interpretive stance
Presentation	A combination of narrative and tables or figures to represent relationships.	Generally narrative form.
Examples	See appendix for a list of studies	(Bair and Hawath's 2005 publications using 'meta-synthesis' and Dixon-Woods et al.'s 2006 publication employing 'critical interpretive synthesis'.)

studies can adapt approaches like ours for their own ends. We believe that such efforts can only result in more critical and methodologically grounded syntheses. Applying systematic and rigorous approaches can only enhance the work that synthesists do.

Growing use of qualitative synthesis approaches among social scientists

Even though qualitative research synthesis is a relatively new addition to the researcher's toolkit, arguably because of its potential benefits, it has seen growing use among social scientists, particularly during this millennium. More than 150 qualitative syntheses have been developed in a range of fields related to professional practice disciplines, most of which have been published within the last decade.

Among the most prominent are health professions, particularly nursing, education, social work and organizational studies. In short, those fields that seek to develop evidence-based policies and practices are adopting the approach. These early efforts highlight the potential of the method and the likelihood of long term growth and acceptance. We outline some of the uses in various fields in this section.

Health profession

The health professions have readily adopted qualitative research synthesis as a research approach, in large part due to the drive for evidence-based practice and policy (Sandelowski and Barroso, 2007). Many in the health professions describe the knowledge that these qualitative research syntheses generate (Finfgeld, 2003; Kearney, 2001; McCormick *et al.*, 2003; Paterson and Thorne, 2003; Sherwood, 1999; Thorne *et al.*, 2004). The health profession literature provides many details about methods for analysis and synthesis of qualitative research (Paterson *et al.*, 2001; Sandelowski and Barroso, 2002a, 2002b, 2003a, 2003b; 2003c; 2003d).

Among health professions, the field of nursing has demonstrated great interest and enthusiasm for the approach and qualitative research synthesis is one of the most commonly used research approaches (Bondas and Hall, 2007). Among the topics that have been examined are issues of access to healthcare (see for example Dixon-Woods *et al.*, 2006) issues of care of patients with various conditions (see for example Carroll, 2004; Martisen *et al.*, 2007), and women's health and motherhood issues (see for example, Aagaard and Hall, 2008; Attree, 2004a, 2004b, 2005a, 2005b; Beck, 2002a, 2002b).

Education

Education is a field that was a leader in the development of the approach, with Noblit and Hare's pioneering work. Despite this initial groundbreaking effort, qualitative research synthesis remains relatively rare in the field of education.

The approach represents an important tool for education researchers, however, who have come under criticism for serving only the interest of researchers without thought to improving practice and policy. Synthesis approaches like qualitative research synthesis can help educators develop cumulative knowledge and thus advance evidence-based policies and practices (Davies, 2000).

Since Noblit and Hare's original work (1988), though relatively few studies have undertaken such an approach, interest in qualitative research synthesis has been on the rise, and important advances have been made. The approach has been used to study particular results of approaches to teaching and learning (Savin-Baden and Major, 2007; Savin-Baden et al., 2008; Scruggs et al., 2007) and processes in particular types of institutions (Rice, 2002), as well as the intersection of various factors on administrator and leadership roles (Pielstick, 1998; Skrla et al., 2001).

Social and community practice

Like other practice professions, those professions dedicated to improving social and community practice have much to gain from such an approach, and indeed some researchers are beginning to employ it. Qualitative research synthesis is being used increasingly in social work and community-based practice professions, in particular to investigate a number of important policy issues. Among those issues are alleviating poverty (Glasmeier and Farrigan, 2005), information distribution during crisis (Duggan and Banwell, 2004) and young mothers and social inequity (McDermott and Graham, 2005).

Organizational studies

Qualitative research synthesis can be exceedingly useful in helping to sort out the mass of literature dealing with organization theory and change. For this reason, important work relying upon qualitative research synthesis also has begun in the area of organizational studies. Among other topics, researchers have used qualitative research synthesis to help investigate individual and organizational strategies for change (Himam, 2002) and management practices (Denyer and Tranfield, 2006. The method has great potential in this field, as in many of the other professions.

Conclusion

In this chapter, we have described some of what we believe are the most common uses of research. We have argued that these approaches fall along a continuum of criticality. To further summarize and support our argument, we offer Table 2.3 that provides a brief overview of these approaches and their critical features and elements.

Table 2.3 Uses of existing studies in science and social science research

Presentation	Reports that provide context for another work		Stand-alone reports that combine evidence			
Category	Literature summary	Literature review	Research review	Research analysis	Research synthesis	Research interpretation
Use	Research as information	Research as justification	Research as demonstration	Research as account	Research as part of whole	Research as representation
Objective	To describe knowledge about a given topic	To explain the space for a research study	To develop a comprehensive picture of knowledge about a topic or issue	To break down findings into essential elements	To aggregate information from a body of studies into a new whole.	To answer a research question by interpreting findings to uncover meaning and generate new knowledge
Level of criticality	Synopsis	Discussion	Discovery	Analysis	Synthesis	Interpretation
Form examples	Annotated bibliography Chronologic summary Methodology summary Thematic summary	Critical/thematic review of relevant research	Thematic reviews Narrative reviews Integrative reviews Systematic reviews	Quantitative meta-analysis Thematic analysis	Quantitative content analysis 'Qualitative' meta analysis Qualitative comparative analysis Case survey Realist synthesis Narrative synthesis	Qualitative research synthesis or meta-ethnography Critical interpretive synthesis or meta-synthesis

Literature of interest	Research report; theoretical papers, evaluation studies, other literature reviews	Research reports along with theoretical papers, evaluation studies, other literature reviews	Research findings from either or both qualitative and quantitative studies	Research findings from quantitative studies	Research findings from either qualitative or quantitative studies	Research findings from qualitative studies or both qualitative and quantitative
Search strategy	Comprehensive review	Selective review of relevant literature	Comprehensive review	Comprehensive review	Comprehensive review	Selective review, to point of saturation
Appraisal of literature	None	Appraisal of fitness of research methods	Appraisal of fitness of research methods	Appraisal of fitness of research methods	Appraisal of fitness of research methods	Appraisals for topic, methods and quality, but accepting that weaker studies have something to offer
Data extracted	Key points	Key points and findings	Key findings	Key findings	Key findings	Key concepts, themes, metaphors
Method of synthesis	Summary	Mapping and gapping/ the matrix method	Analysing findings from many studies	Analysing findings from many studies	Aggregation into whole	Interpretation: constant comparison; refutational synthesis, reciprocal translation, line of argument

Continued

Table 2.3. Cont'd

Presentation	Reports that provide context for another work		Stand-alone reports that combine evidence			
Key components in presentation	Literature is described in narrative form, usually one source at a time	Literature is presented as an overview and justification for the planned study	Literature is presented in narrative form, grouped thematically	Literature is presented in tabular form	Literature is presented in tabular or narrative form.	Literature is presented in the following steps: 1st order analysis 2nd order synthesis 3rd order interpretation
Data presentation	Abstract or summary narrative	Narrative	Narrative	Charts and tables	Narrative with charts and tables	Narrative with tables and figures

These various approaches share the common feature of using research literature. They also build upon each other. Each step along the continuum requires having completed the steps before it so that, to do an interpretation, one must necessarily have reviewed, analysed and synthesized the literature. However, we note that we do not believe that the continuum is finished. We believe that we are still striving for a critical interpretive approach to combining evidence. It is this belief that has driven our own research and that has encouraged our work in this text.

For us, qualitative research synthesis represents an important way to manage and make sense of existing qualitative studies. We see the process as methodologically grounded and rigorous and thus as having great potential to add to the development of professional practice and theory. It is an approach, however, that must be undertaken with care. It is not a simple or easy method. Indeed, Thorne *et al.* (2002) suggest that it is critical not to underestimate the complexity of synthesis approaches. In fact, they require analysis of theoretical, methodological and contextual foundations that they state are 'not to be undertaken by the inexperienced or the faint of the heart' (p. 449) and stress that the 'time-consuming and messy' aspects of qualitative research are not avoided by a synthesis approach (Thorne *et al.*, 2004: 1343). We argue further that these aspects are intensified by the approach. For this reason, we describe the processes of the approach in more detail in Part 2 of this book.

Part 2

Doing qualitative research synthesis

Chapter 3

Designing the synthesis

In this chapter, we describe the key processes associated with designing and defining the parameters of the search during qualitative research synthesis. We argue that the synthesist should be self-aware throughout this design process. We believe that it is critical, for example, to acknowledge the interplay between synthesist and study during the question design process, since the question sets the parameters for what will and will not be studied. Further, the way in which a synthesist defines search strings, locates studies, articulates inclusion and exclusion criteria, and then evaluates articles, all are central to qualitative research synthesis, and all are influenced heavily by the synthesist's belief systems. For these reasons, we believe that it is critical for the synthesist to be self-aware, to the point of self-consciousness, while establishing search parameters.

Being self-conscious as a synthesist

Conducting a synthesis necessitates self-consciousness from a private as well as public perspective. From a private perspective, it is critical to acknowledge that preconceived ideas and notions directly affect decisions. It is therefore important to be aware of your belief systems and to consider how they will influence choices. From a public perspective, it is important to be explicit in describing the design and acknowledging those influences and interactions so that the reader can review the design of the study from an informed perspective. Thus it is particularly important to be self-conscious during the design phase.

There is no formula by which a self-conscious design may be accomplished. We argue, however, that by following a well charted path and asking self-reflective critical questions along the way, the synthesist can move toward self-awareness and thus ultimately achieve a more rigorous and robust study. An overview of this process may be seen in Figure 3.1.

Formulating a question

Developing a clear and bounded question is one of the most important tasks that a synthesist faces for a number of reasons. First, the synthesist demonstrates

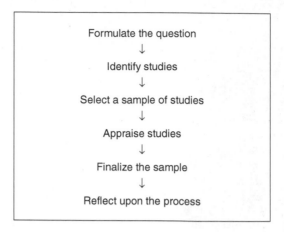

Figure 3.1 Defining the search parameters.

knowledge of the discipline or field through the articulation of a cogent question. Second, a good question determines what knowledge will be accumulated as well as produced through the synthesis process. The question, then, in many ways determines what the answers will be. Third, a good question and resultant knowledge determines what will happen next – what future research will be conducted and what practices and policies will be changed as a result.

Due to these reasons, the design of a question for a synthesis should not be taken lightly. Indeed, questions have the power to improve the human condition by informing knowledge and shaping wisdom. Yet, question design is a complicated task, which often occurs, we believe, at almost a subconscious level. We argue for making the question design and development a more visible and self-aware process.

Considering the purpose of the question

Frequently researchers are asked to consider the question of 'what do you want to know' in designing research. This question, of course, drives the research forward, from determining who or what will be studied, what the methods will be for collecting data, and what the approach for data analysis will be. It is a critical question worthy of time and attention. Few researchers, though, are encouraged to go beyond this initial question to a consideration of the equally important question of 'why do you want to know that?' or 'what is the impact of such a study likely to be on policy and practice?' Yet these are the kind of questions that should be at the very heart of qualitative research synthesis. While these may not be the questions that drive every methodological decision, they are certainly the questions that drive interpretive ones. If synthesists for example, wish to interrogate the data (as suggested by Walsh and Downe, 2005) from conflicting reports to determine what forces are at play, they necessarily assume the role of critic or judge. If, however, synthesists design a question in order to open up new insights and understandings about data (as again Walsh indicates is a potential purpose of a synthesis), then they likely are to assume the role of analyst. Finally, if synthesists wish to argue for a particular interpretation or application of the data or findings, and align themselves with the data, juxtaposed with theory and inference, then they are likely to assume the role of advocate.

All of the above are legitimate purposes for undertaking a synthesis, and in many ways parallel Noblit and Hare's (1988) suggestions for positioning studies themselves. However, we argue that in isolation, any of the three leave open the potential for misuse. We believe that the synthesist rather should take on the three different roles at various times in order to achieve all three purposes simultaneously. This can be done by questioning the data in interpretations from the various perspectives, then resolving the results into a more complete interpretation, attempting to convey as transparent an interpretation as possible to the audience.

Identifying origins of ideas for important questions

A question for a qualitative research synthesis generally develops from one three main areas, all of which should be considered from a critical perspective.

1   The synthesist's interest in a given question most is often the starting point (see Beck, 2002a, 2002b; Paterson *et al.*, 2001, 2003; Paterson and Thorne, 2003).
2   Problems of practice often serve as the springboard, especially in professional education. These problems often are found explicated in professional newspapers, magazines, etc.
3   Previous research can, and does, serve as a springboard for a synthesis. An existing meta-analysis often is a good starting point, as qualitative studies generally have not been considered as a part of that work. Findings from meta-summaries often are a foundation for qualitative synthesis projects (See Noblit and Hare, 1998 and Sandelowski, 2006).

Perhaps most importantly, it is critical to begin question design by taking stock of existing literature. Scanning abstracts of existing research articles can give synthesists a general idea of the kinds of questions that have been asked previously – arguably a key component for any kind of research, but even more so for syntheses, since finding a sufficient number of articles will depend on basing a question on the questions that have already been examined. Such a scan involves surveying the field around a topic, reviewing the questions that have been asked, and making some sense of them.

There are many things to consider related to the way in which question origins can influence a synthesis. The availability of papers on a given topic area can influence the nature of the synthesis. When relying upon previous literature, many times findings from original studies (or meta-analyses or meta-summaries) have been influenced by the researcher who undertook them. Thus these researcher intentions should also be considered when determining a question.

Identifying clear question components

Some synthesis scholars have argued that particularly when developing evidence-based practice, there are several key components to consider when developing a question. Such questions may include concepts such as the following: person, intervention, environment, stakeholders, comparison and outcome (see for example, Armstrong, 1999; Richardson *et al.*, 1995; Schlosser *et al.* 2007). We explain these characteristics more fully in the following table (Table 3.1). We also give an example from our 2007 (Savin-Baden and Major, 2007) article in which we considered the components as we developed our question.

Table 3.1 Components of a good question

	Issue to be considered	Example: Savin-Baden and Major (2007)
Person	The individual and their membership in a group, whether demographic, social or other	Faculty who had changed their teaching practices
Environment	The context in which the person exists	Institutions of higher education
Intervention	The programme, test or other condition to which the individual or individuals have been exposed	Moving from lecturing to a problem-based learning approach
Comparison	The unit of change that is critical to consider, whether it is between a control group versus experimental group, an intervention versus no intervention or other, a before and after, or other	Changes between who they were before and who they became after using problem-based learning
Outcome	The change that has occurred, whether positive or negative	Shifts in teacher knowledge and teacher stance

Ultimately the guiding question for our synthesis became: how do university faculty who move from lecturing to problem-based learning change? Just small adjustments to question components, however, would have fundamentally altered the study design, the articles included, the inclusion and exclusion criteria, and ultimately the findings. Consider how our study would have been changed if we had looked at the components in Table 3.2 instead.

Table 3.2 Possible alterations to study design

Person	Faculty who had changed their teaching practices.
Environment	Institutions of higher education
Intervention	Moving from lecturing to a problem-based learning approach.
Comparison	Attitudes about problem-based learning
Outcome	Chances of continued use of the approach

Our question would have been something more like the following: How does the experience of adopting problem-based learning influence college or university faculty likelihood of continuation of the approach. In the former, we were interested in learning about and informing others about how an intervention ultimately shapes faculty. Had we done the latter, we would have discovered how change influences staff preferences for an instructional approach. Thus minor changes in question make significant differences in a study.

It is important, then, for the synthesist to identify the most critical components of the question and to be careful in selection of variables, which will influence the direction of the study. Furthermore, the synthesist should be careful to consider why these variables were selected. Finally, the synthesist should consider what is being left out and why through selection of variables.

Reflecting upon research question

After developing the research question, it is important to consider the nature of the question, from both a process and product perspective. We offer two sets of considerations. The first involves using questions that can help the synthesist to reflect upon the role assumed when creating the question and the purpose of the question itself. A 'question set' that can guide decisions in developing a question and allow a synthesist to be more self-aware. Table 3.3 is a starting point.

Table 3.3 Self-reflective questions for question development

Question purpose	Why am I developing the question in the first place?
	What knowledge is to be gained by conducting the synthesis?
	What problem can be solved?
	What do I hope to accomplish?
	Why do I want to accomplish this?
Question source	From where did the idea for the question germinate?
	What experiences led me to this question?
	What do I believe the answer to this question is?
Question components	Which variables are the most important to consider for the synthesis?
	What variables are the ones that are selected?
	What does the selection of these variables do to delimit the study?
	Why should this delimitation be done?

In addition to the self-reflective question set that we have proposed, we also believe that there are several practical questions about the viability and efficacy of the study that the synthesist should address prior to beginning work. These are as follows.

1   Is the question related to an innovative topic?

- Is the issue or topic of professional interest to me and to an audience of my peers?
- Is the topic an area of importance in my field?

2   Is the question clear?

- Are all of the components clear?
- Is the wording appropriate and jargon-free?

3   Is it possible to answer the question through qualitative research synthesis?

- Can the question be answered qualitatively?
- Do a sufficient number of original studies that are related to this question exist?
- Is the scope of this question reasonable? (e.g. is it broad enough to allow me to gather a pool of studies but narrow enough not to generate thousands of articles?)
- Are the articles accessible?

Identifying studies

Searching for and retrieving qualitative studies can be a challenge, so a key characteristic of qualitative synthesis is the use of explicit searching strategies, with the researcher providing a clear account of the search for, and selection of, relevant evidence. One of the main rationales for providing so much detail is to create an audit or paper trail so that strategies may be reproduced by others. We also believe that being explicit can help keep the researcher in a reflexive frame of mind and can inform the intended audience about the decision making strategies that went into the development of the synthesis. We believe that there are several key phases during study identification in which synthesists must be particularly self-aware about their interaction with the design: setting the parameters for source materials, determining the search strings, setting inclusion and exclusion criteria, and appraising the studies.

Setting parameters for the source materials

Determining the sources from which existing research reports are drawn is a decision that is worth considered attention. Most qualitative syntheses use studies from peer-reviewed journals, since these have been subjected to peer review and thus have at least one layer of quality control built in. However, different journals may range greatly in the rigour of the peer review process, so this criterion may, or may not, have that much value. A few projects have used unpublished studies (the so called 'grey literature'). There is justification for using unpublished studies, since they may contain rich, thick description sometimes lacking in published works that must meet minimum page length (Beck, 2002b). Whatever approach the synthesist chooses, it is a good idea to be explicit about the rationale for selecting it.

Defining the search process

Online databases, such as Educational Resources Information Center's (ERIC), Academic Search Elite and Google Scholar serve as useful starting points. They do not eliminate the need for hand-searching tables of contents of key journals in addition to bibliographies of relevant articles. Further, reviewing Listservs and other relevant mailing lists, and searching the Cochrane networks can provide additional data. Whatever approach taken, it is doubtful that every publication in existence will be located. The information explosion and current indexing systems simply will not allow it. The job of the synthesist simply is to plan a search to yield the most possible relevant articles for initial consideration.

Determining the search strings

Another decision that necessarily alters the constitution of the study involves the search strings that the synthesist uses to return information. It is important to ensure that search terms are clear and focused. During the search and particularly the electronic phase, it is important to use Boolean logic and to divine the appropriate mix. In most databases, such as ERIC or Academic Search Elite, it is possible to make good use of connectors in order to extend or limit a search. To find articles about learning, for example, connectors like the following may be used to further streamline the search:

'AND' (Learning AND)
'OR' (Learning OR)
'AND NOT' (Learning NOT)

Parentheses can also be used when conducting an advanced search. For example: *education AND (schools OR college)* – this expresses a search for records containing information about education schools or colleges. Synthesists should again be clear on what they are including as well as leaving out.

The issue that most synthesists will face, rather than not identifying enough studies to begin with, is limiting the search in a meaningful way. In Savin-Baden and McFarland's article (2007), for example, they returned nearly 6,000 articles from using a combination of the following search terms:

> Academic practice, leadership; Communities; Discipline–based pedagogy; Education-based development; E-learning; Higher education; Influence; Interprofessional education; Knowledge management; Knowledge transfer; Phenomenology; Policy development; Problem-based learning; Qualitative research; Reflective practice; Teaching and learning; Transfer

Clearly 6,000 results is an unmanageable number of articles. The synthesists's task then, becomes how to deal with articles in these numbers and return a usable set. Savin-Baden and McFarland accomplished this goal by reading the abstracts of these studies in order to locate those that were qualitative and that had thick description. Although scanning in this way can be time-consuming, it enables the synthesist to gain quality articles at the outset and offers an opportunity to discover exactly what is and is not available.

Determining inclusion and exclusion criteria

One of the synthesist's key roles is to decide whether findings across studies are comparable and compatible (Noblit and Hare, 1988). In order to make this determination, the synthesist generally sets surface parameters in order to assess comparability of findings (Sandelowski *et al.*, 1997). However, scholars have differing opinions about what should be considered when making decisions. As we noted in Chapter 1, some synthesists, for example, suggest not including studies that use different qualitative methods (Estabrooks *et al.*, 1994; Jensen and Allen, 1994, 1996; Sherwood, 1999). Others believe that any studies with findings that may be combined can be included (Sandelowski *et al.*, 1997). The synthesist must make these determinations based upon the purpose of the study.

There are several factors though upon which most scholar-synthesists agree. It is important in qualitative research synthesis, for example, that included studies contain qualitative data, rather than simply summaries of themes. All also seem to agree that it important to limit the study by topic and research question. Most seem to agree that it is important to set some timeframe (even if it is a long one, it is important to identify it). When first undertaking qualitative synthesis it is often difficult to judge what is realistic. There is often an assumption that the timescale be narrow, yet at times a wide one (for example, ten years) is needed to ensure that a sufficient number of quality articles are located.

In addition to the other criteria, we recommend that the synthesist search for articles that meet the following baseline standards.

1   Articles contain data in the form of thick quotations/descriptions from the primary data set.
2   The methods of data collection, handling and analysis are clear.
3   Primary researchers have made some acknowledgement of their stance.

Table 3.4 Inclusion and exclusion criteria

Criteria	Include studies	Exclude studies
Topic		
Research question		
Date		
Research design		
Researcher stance		
Included data		
Publication outlet		

We find it important in qualitative research synthesis that the included studies present qualitative data, otherwise it not possible to undertake analysis and synthesis phases. We find that methods must be clear to determine whether they are methodologically consistent, even if not exactly the same. Finally, we believe it critical that the original researchers have acknowledged stance to allow for data interpretations from an informed perspective. These elements, we find, are essential for including articles into the synthesis in a meaningful way. Inclusion and exclusion criteria should be constructed, stated, recorded and applied. A form like that in Table 3.4 may be used to help guide decisions of fit.

Reflection on identifying articles

We recommend using the question set in Table 3.5 for considering how an initial set of articles will be selected for the qualitative synthesis.

Table 3.5 Selecting articles

Setting parameters for the source material	Will I use only published studies or also draw from grey material?
	What does my selection mean will be included?
	What will be left out?
Setting parameters for the search process	What methods am I using to search?
	Are my connectors limiting or extending my search appropriately?
	What am I by design leaving out?
Identifying the search strings	What other search strings might I use?
	How would including them change the nature of the synthesis?
Determining inclusion and exclusion criteria	How does imposing the criteria I set influence what articles are left out?
	How can I justify these decisions?

Appraising quality of studies

Appraising study quality also is important. We recognize that not every study will be of equal quality. Some will have a great deal to offer, but through interpretation and inclusion of an ample supply of original data, others simply will be weaker. Such weaker studies may still be of value though, if they have something to add to the synthesis or something of value that enhances the synthesist's ability to interpret data. However, a study that has design flaws can lead to the drawing of faulty conclusions and thus interfere with interpretation. So while it is imperative not to discount a weaker study, it is also essential to exclude studies that are fatally flawed. Table 3.6, adapted from a process advocated by the Joanna Briggs Institute (2007), a non-profit research organization dedicated to studying evidence-based practices for health care professionals, is an example of a guide to such decisions.

Table 3.6 A guide to inclusion and exclusion decisions

Criteria for appraisal	Response	
There is acknowledgement of researcher stance	Yes	No
There is congruity between researcher stance and methodology	Yes	No
There is congruity between methodology and research goals.	Yes	No
There is congruity between research goals and research questions	Yes	No
There is congruity between research questions and data collection techniques	Yes	No
There is congruity between research questions and data analysis	Yes	No
There is congruity between research questions and presentation of findings	Yes	No
There is congruity between methodology and interpretation of findings	Yes	No

Adapted from the JBI QARI Critical Appraisal Checklist for Interpretive and Critical Research at the Joanna Briggs Institute.

Thus, the selection of quality appraisal criteria ultimately affects the constitution of the synthesis.

Reflecting upon assessment criteria

In applying assessment of quality criteria, it is important to consider what is a 'signal' in the original studies and seeing through the 'noise' of methodological issues. Due to the critical nature of assessment of the qualitative of articles, we recommend that the synthesist use great care when making a decision to exclude an article based upon quality. The synthesis may wish to consider the reflective questions listed in Table 3.7 prior to excluding studies.

Table 3.7 Reflective questions to user prior to excluding studies

Determining the quality assessment criteria	How might applying these criteria cause me to miss important data? Are the criteria important enough to my rationale to justify this potential exclusion?

Selecting the final sample

Many questions surround the selection of a final sample of studies, and often reviewers will question how such a decision has been made, particularly if the final sample is small. The synthesist should spend time justifying the decision. We believe that there are two critical issues for discussion, both of which we believe involve finding a balance between two extremes. The first includes whether to strive for a comprehensive sample or to seek studies to the point of saturation. The second involves striving for a number that allows for maximum richness of data while still remaining manageable for data analysis.

Comprehensiveness versus saturation

Some synthesists argue for a comprehensive sample. The arguments for such a stance are strong. One of the objects of conducting a synthesis, after all, is to develop a comprehensive bibliography of a phenomenon. Others argue that it is important to reach saturation (Booth, 2006). We believe it is important to bridge these two perspectives. We think it is important to initially identify as many articles as possible. Yet as qualitative researchers, we argue for the position that it is critical to sample to the point of achieving saturation – although we suggest that on another level 'saturation' is also somewhat of a misnomer with so many new articles being published daily. However, when during the data analysis, it becomes clear that fewer and fewer themes are recurring then a form of temporary saturation will have been reached and thus it is not important to continue analysing articles simply for the sake of finding additional justification of a theme's existence.

Richness versus manageability

Some synthesists strive for a comprehensive sample of studies, arguably because they believe that they will have a richer data set from which to draw.

However, the larger the number of studies available the more that can be developed, particularly along the lines of theory (Kearney, 2001). Further, the more original data strings there are, the easier it is to find strong exemplars of themes. We argue that at some point, the data set becomes too large for analysis, synthesis and interpretation in the iterative way we have outlined in Chapter 4.

Furthermore, since each study should be 'rich' with information, synthesists typically have recommended including a small number of studies, from 2–4 (Noblit and Hare, 1988), although some have indicated that as many as 10–20 is acceptable. Our own work suggests that between 6 and 10 studies is optimal to provide sufficient yet manageable data.

Reflecting upon study selection

In our work, we have determined that it is appropriate and desirable to apply a set of self reflective questions focused on study selection. We outline these questions in Table 3.8.

Table 3.8 Self-reflective question set for selecting studies

Saturation	Have the same themes begun to reappear?
	Is anything new showing up in the studies that requires sampling to continue?
Setting a number	How can setting a specific number be justified?
	Does the number of studies identified provide sufficient original data for analysis?
	Should a number be set?

Final reflection upon design process

We have identified the key phases of the design and article selection process and have argued that it is critical at each phase to reflect upon the process through consistent questioning of interests, processes and products. We further argue that it is critical to take a final moment for reflection prior to beginning data analysis, synthesis and interpretation. We believe that this reflection upon the design can occur in three key phases (following Glassick *et al.*, 1997):

1 critical appraisal of work;
2 supporting appraisal with evidence;
3 using reflection to plan future work.

We offer the following advice about how to accomplish these phases.

1) Critical appraisal of work: In this phase, the synthesist may wish to reflect upon the state of knowledge around the topic selected, considering what questions

have been asked and whether the overarching question has represented a point of commonality among the existing literature. It is important to reflect upon whether the search process represents the state of the art in technological sophistication and whether due diligence in hand searching to identify the work that is available has been done. It is important to consider whether the appraisal criteria represent current best practices in qualitative research.

2) Supporting appraisal with evidence: In supporting the critical appraisal of work with evidence, the synthesist may wish to find support in the literature to bolster claims made. For example, a policy brief or white paper that identified critical questions in the literature would be an excellent source for justifying selection of a question. A recent publication outlining advances in electronic search technology can be an assurance that the best use of resources has been made. A national or international collaboration that has adopted appraisal criteria (such as we used above), or even a methods paper that discusses criteria for assuring rigour of a study, could be a good guide for helping support selection of quality appraisal criteria.

3) Using reflection to plan future work: Finally, true reflection arguably can occur when a synthesist determines what might be done the same or differently the next time the task of synthesis design and study selection is undertaken. Considering what went well and what could be improved in the future will enable sense to be made of where the process held up well under scrutiny and where weaknesses were evident.

We believe that in large part, reflection is for the benefit of the synthesist and provides the assurance that a well designed study has been crafted, which will allow data analysis to move forward in ways that will be valued. We also believe, however, that providing information about the reflection process in the methods section of the paper can help the synthesist establish a level of credibility with the reader. For this reason, we recommend that the synthesist in particular provide the information contained in number 2 above, the evidence that supports the claims of critical reflection, while planning the study design. For example, noting that an established instrument was adapted for evaluating studies can help the reader have confidence in those decisions.

Conclusion

In this chapter, we have argued that the synthesist should engage in a self-conscious design. There are several key points in which the synthesist must make important decisions that will necessarily guide the constitution of the study. We recommend applying a set of self-reflective questions during critical decision-making points both during the research synthesis and again at the end. This rigour will produce a more plausible study; however, a scrupulous process of analysing, synthesizing, and interpreting studies also is required, which we present and explore in detail in Chapter 4.

Analysing, synthesizing and interpreting studies

Introduction

There is a general lack of information about how qualitative research synthesis is undertaken, so in this chapter, we articulate processes for analysis, synthesis and interpretation of data. The steps of moving from analysis to synthesis and on into interpretations often are found to be complex and demanding. In order to help ensure this process is as straightforward as possible, this chapter offers an approach for undertaking this task. While we demonstrate it as a structured process here, it is important to note that we advocate, as do others, what is in many ways an 'iterative process of thinking, interpreting, creating, theorizing and reflecting' (Paterson *et al.*, 2001: 112). Figure 4.1 provides an overview of the processes we outline in this chapter.

We further suggest that this process of analysis, synthesis and interpretation requires transparency: a best effort to be clear and explicit about our work. While it is important to also be transparent in design as well as in presenting and disseminating findings, we believe it is of particular importance in the analysis, synthesis and interpretation phase.

Beginning the process

Several specific steps can help to ensure a sound beginning. We assert that synthesists should follow several steps to prepare for analysis. Among these are situating studies, deciding what will count as data, comparing studies, and identifying findings from studies.

Considering how studies may be situated

Determining how to view the studies together is a critical element of qualitative research synthesis. Noblit and Hare (1988) propose three ways to order the studies.

1   Studies can be combined and one study is presented in terms of another. This allows for studies to be directly compared. In this *reciprocal translation analysis*, the researcher identifies key metaphors, themes or concepts and translates them into each other. The synthesist makes judgments about the

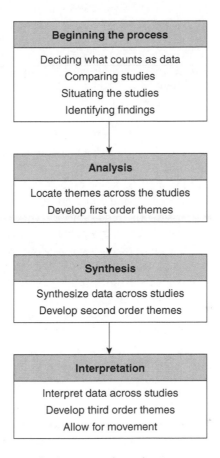

Figure 4.1 The processes involved in research synthesis.

ability of one study's concepts to capture the concepts from another and selects the 'most adequate' to describe the phenomenon.

2   Studies may be set against one another. In this way, one study can serve to refute another. In this *refutational synthesis*, the researcher characterizes and attempts to explain contradictions between the separate studies.

3   Studies may be tied to one another through noting how one study informs another (Noblit and Hare, 1988). The studies represent a *line of argument*, which are

  a   emic, or analysing structural and functional elements;
  b   historical, or using chronology to provide order;
  c   comparative, or using an analogy of the relationships between the studies;
  d   holistic, interpreting the systems of belief through interpretations and contexts.

The importance of situating the studies enables synthesists to build and present a general interpretation that is grounded in findings from the original studies in order to identify the themes that most powerfully represent the entire dataset (Dixon-Woods *et al.*, 2006). We feel that it is critical to consider these potential positions prior to analysis, synthesis and interpretation in order to better understand the processes as they occur.

Deciding what will count as data

Synthesists differ on what counts as data from primary studies and in so doing, they tend to fall along a continuum of beliefs. At one end of the continuum, some argue that everything from the study title to the discussion counts as data and should be considered since all could contain important messages (following Noblit and Hare, 1988). At the other end, authors argue for stricter adherence to only original data presented in the findings for synthesis, as evident in many published articles. Synthesists should determine which position will be followed and provide a justification for the decision. We suggest that there is middle ground, whereby the context of the study is important and can aid synthesis and interpretation, but argue that at this preliminary stage, the primary focus is to ensure that the studies contain rich, thick description in the form of quotations from the original data, which are essential for data analysis.

Comparing studies

Each of the selected papers should be read through in order to record the details of the study including the setting, participants, notions of validity and positioning of the researcher as well as to identify the main concepts. A summary of the studies may be prepared to illustrate the relative similarity of those studies used and indicate, in terms of both methodology and findings, how they coalesce in ways that will provide a useful qualitative synthesis. Such a summary is shown in Box 4.1.

Once the articles have been summarized it is then possible to create a tabulated summary, as is in Table 4.1

This kind of table can further facilitate a direct comparison of articles. In our own work, we have found such tables useful for providing a graphic organizer of key study components. We provide a completed example in Table 4.2.

Identifying findings

It is important to begin a synthesis by identifying findings from the primary studies, which we believe happens in four ways: locating, extracting, evaluating, and translating findings. Locating findings requires reading the studies carefully and identifying clear findings that relate to the research question. Findings not related to the central research question should be discarded.

Extracting findings is the process of deconstructing the studies in order to compare them. It requires isolating or working back to fundamental processes

Box 4.1 Exemplar of summary of studies

The first study (Major and Palmer, 2006) draws from the research pool of the 31 faculty members involved in the grant-funded project to implement problem-based learning across the university. This study examined the process of transforming faculty knowledge through in-depth face-to-face interviews. Researchers found that faculty existing knowledge and the institutional intervention influenced new knowledge of faculty roles, student roles, disciplinary structures and pedagogy brought about by adopting problem-based learning. Communicating new knowledge solidified the transformation.

The second study (Wilkie, 2004) explored the espoused and actual conceptions of facilitation adopted by a group of nursing lecturers on an undergraduate nursing programme in the UK that utilized problem-based learning. The research followed a group of 18 nursing lecturers over a three-year period as they implemented problem-based learning within a three-year Diploma of Higher Education in Nursing programme. The research design was situated within a constructivist interpretivist paradigm. The constructivist approach is concerned with understanding and reconstructing, rather than explaining or predicting. Findings indicated four approaches to facilitation; however, the approaches were neither fixed nor hierarchical but were time and context dependent in relation to factors associated with students, with the problem-based learning material or in response to changes in the facilitators themselves.

The third study (Foord-May, 2006) examined faculty experience of the implementation of problem-based learning in a physiotherapy programme. Basic qualitative interview methods were used to understanding faculty perspectives and data were collected. The study relied on semi-structured interviews with seven faculty. Data were analysed using the constant comparative method and nine themes emerged that related to faculty perceptions of change and the required support for the implementation of an innovation such as problem-based learning.

Table 4.1 Summary of studies

Methods, perceptions and concepts	Article 1	Article 2	Article 3	Article 4	Article 5	And so on...
Sample						
Setting						
Methods						
Data collection						
Notion of validity						
Positioning of researcher						
Main themes and concepts indentified by study authors						

Table 4.2 Comparison of articles

Methods, perceptions and concepts	Savin-Baden (2000)	Major and Palmer (2002)	Major and Palmer (2006)	Savin-Baden (2003)	Wilkie (2004)	Foord-May (2006)
Sample	22 staff	31 faculty	31 faculty	20 staff	18 staff	7 faculty
Setting	Four departments in four UK universities	Private university in the US	Private university in the US	Faculty in UK university	Faculty in UK University	Department in US University
Methods	New paradigm research and narrative inquiry	Narrative inquiry	Narrative inquiry	Narrative and collaborative inquiry	Constructivist interpretivist paradigm	Qualitative inquiry
Data collection	Semi-structured interviews	Semi-structured interviews	Semi-structured interviews	In-depth interviews, email discussions	Semi-structured interviews, audio taping of seminars	Semi-structured interviews; focus groups
Notion of validity	Trustworthiness and reflexivity	Trustworthiness and reflexivity	Trustworthiness and reflexivity	Trustworthiness and reflexivity	Trustworthiness and reflexivity	Participant validation
Positioning of researcher	Inquirer and reflexive learner	Inquirers and Insider/outsider	Inquirers and Insider/outsider	Co-inquirer	Co-inquirer	Inquirer and researcher
Main themes and concepts identified by study authors	Disjunction causes faculty change in pedagogical stance	Faculty knowledge of students is fundamentally altered with adoption of PBL	Faculty knowledge of discipline and pedagogy is altered with PBL and ultimately expressed differently	Pedagogical stance affects positioning of faculty in PBL environments	Facilitator approaches are affected by conceptions of learning	Support for faculty is vital for effective change management

used in the original research in order to unpack what is initially taken as given. Much of the work in extracting findings requires identifying thick description that can be used during analysis.

One of the traps that is easy to fall into is to accept findings from the original studies at face value. Yet often such findings are not supported by evidence. The primary researchers pronounce a finding and the reader is to believe them. Ensuring that findings are documented and supported will help establish the rigour of the study. Findings, then, may be assessed for levels of integrity. We recommend developing and using a rating schedule, similar to that in Table 4.3, which we adapted from a template used at The Joanna Briggs Institute (2007).

Table 4.3 A rating schedule to establish rigour of findings

Unequivocal	Findings supported with clear and compelling evidence
Credible	Findings that are plausible given the weight of evidence
Unsupported	Findings that are suggested but not supported by data

Those findings that meet the levels of 'unequivocal' or 'credible' may be considered to constitute findings or themes.

Similar findings then are translated into a common language. For example, in our 2007 article, we reviewed the findings from the original studies about staff experiences with problem-based learning. We noted key concepts and themes that stood out amongst the studies and labelled these, often using the words of the staff interviewed. Table 4.4 presents an example.

Table 4.4 Identifying findings from data

Text	Our translation
The course went from probably 75 to 80% lecture ... and then it completely flipped. ... the biggest change that occurred there is that you remove yourself from the position of being the sole deliverer of information and being the lecturer who stands in front and dispenses and you really have to give up and sacrifice your control over the class in that way. So not walking in prepared to deliver a lecture, I shouldn't say not being prepared, but not expecting to deliver it and having the pieces of the problem that you want them to work on is a very different mindset each time you go in the classroom	Staff shifted from lecturer to facilitator

This example demonstrates the translation process, beginning with the raw data and using the language of the participant. In our case, many of the authors in the original studies had identified the above as either a primary theme or a subtheme.

Analysis

The purpose of analysis is to move beyond comparison in ways that would just provide an overview of the issues or themes that emerged from each study. The analysis of relationships between the studies is a central idea in qualitative research synthesis and involves listing and organizing these themes and attempting to relate them to one another (Schofield, 1990). Analysis requires directly comparing and contrasting narratives of related topics and metaphors and viewing them as in unison or as divergent (Shkedi, 2005; Noblit and Hare, 1988). Analysis then involves:

1   developing first order themes and codes;
2   locating themes across studies.

Developing first order themes and codes

Articles should be examined for the existence of themes from the findings presented in the studies. Rather than just starting with raw data or translations, it also is possible to begin with predetermined themes and descriptions that the original authors had chosen to include. It should be noted that these predetermined themes are used as part of the analysis and may be used in the final interpretations – but they may also be discarded if more relevant themes are found or created.

Just as within primary qualitative research, basic qualitative coding may be used to help facilitate this process. Coding in synthesis serves the same purpose that it does in primary research: labelling findings to assist later retrieval and comparison. We offer the following examples of coding schemes.

- Factual coding: Factual coding, sometimes called descriptive coding, involves coding for concrete facts, including actions, events and processes.
- Conceptual or thematic coding: This is also sometimes called generative or open coding. It involves developing categories out of concepts and themes that are evident in the data. 'Open' in this sense means that synthesists begin data exploration without prior assumptions about what it contains.
- Relational coding: This form of coding, often called axial coding, involves making connections between categories. Connections between categories and subcategories are sought.
- Structural coding: Structural coding, sometimes called selective coding, involves coding for the structural relationship between the categories. In other words, it involves seeking relationships between a given category and its related categories.

- Interpretive coding: In interpretive coding, the synthesist is able to focus on abstract issues and concerns, such as participant perspectives.

A good code is one that has a sufficient number of characters to make it distinguishable from others, that clearly delineates a description of the theme and that can be augmented as subthemes emerge. Coding proceeds until a form of temporary saturation is reached and no new codes are developed in a category.

Identifying first order themes across studies

The next stage of analysis is to examine codes together in order to locate themes that appear across multiple studies, although findings that appear in only one study should be retained so that synthesists can make an assessment of why it did not appear more frequently. Through this process of identifying common themes, not only are data compared and reinterpreted across the studies but also metaphors, ideas, concepts and contexts are explored in order to consider how the findings in the primary studies have been contextualized and presented. This means reading the data carefully and examining the relationship between them while identifying whether the overarching first order themes are present. A matrix with studies on one axis and all potential first order findings on the other, with a checkmark used to indicate when each theme has occurred, can be useful for tracking purposes. Having begun to locate cross-study themes and concepts it will then be possible to move towards synthesizing data.

Synthesis

Synthesis involves the process of combining themes and categories across the studies in order to create a new perspective or view of the issues. It is important at this point to take both a critical and reflexive stance. One of the difficulties with the conception of reflexivity is that how one sees possible combinations depends upon where one is coming from. It is important to remain aware of this difficulty during the process of synthesis. Synthesis includes the following steps:

1 combining themes across the studies;
2 Identifying second order themes across studies.

Combining themes across the studies

Synthesis by definition means taking parts and developing them into a new whole. This stage involves taking the analysis of thick description further, not just locating themes across the studies but also bringing themes from the studies together. It involves combining pre-existing themes and categories across the studies in order to create a new perspective or view of the issues. It sets up the possibility for new understandings which may in turn contribute to increased knowledge. The process in theory looks something like the following:

Theme 1 =>
Theme 2 =>   Composite theme=>
Theme 3 =>

In practice, though, it is a complex process and requires detailed analysis not only of the studies and their data, but also the subtext within and across studies. It is important at this point to ensure that realistic transitions are made between levels of synthesis. Thus, the transition between levels requires continually moving between themes that emerge from analysis and those included in the studies being used.

Identifying second order themes across studies

Annotations, maps, tables and grids can be used to identify and connect studies with the key second order themes to track themes across studies in a relatively straightforward process. For example, tables and grids may be used to help to develop second order categories categorizing articles under the emerging themes and commonalities and recurring themes arising from the different articles, as in the example in Table 4.5.

Interpreting findings

The original argument for meta-ethnography (Noblit and Hare, 1988) is that through interpretation and by acknowledging the positions of the researchers as interpretivists, it is possible to recover the social and theoretical context of the research and thus reveal further noteworthy findings. Interpretation then adds something beyond the mere comparison and aggregation of results from all of the studies. Rather, interpretation involves translating information into something understandable that bears resemblance to the original studies but that takes it to a higher level. Qualitative research synthesis should afford an opportunity to construct an (always contestable) interpretation. Yet developing an interpretation is a complex process. This stage involves

1   seeking revelation;
2   developing third order interpretations;
3   allowing movement.

Seeking revelation

The nature of the process of interpretation often is hidden in qualitative studies and syntheses in particular, yet it is important to consider how it happens.

Table 4.5 Example of identifying second order themes across studies

Themes	Improving practice	Changing practice	Impact of innovation	Creating theory through exploring practice	Student experience	Staff experience
Hara, Kling (2000)	Yes, students distress in web-based distance courses	No	Yes	No	Yes	Yes
Mullins Kiley (2002)	Yes, improve practice of PhD examiners	No	No	Moving towards a model	No	Yes
Lawrie, (2004)	No	Yes	Yes, exploring use of dialogue journal	No	Yes	No
Ashley, Gibson, Daly, Baker, Newton (2006)	Yes, used reflective practice to improve learning in dentistry	No	No	Yes, developed models of good learning	Yes	No
Kreber (2004)	Yes, analysed findings of 2 earlier studies on reflection	No	No	Yes, meta analysis of studies	No	Yes

Consider the following example in which Maggi demonstrates the iterative and cyclical nature of the process of interpretation.

Maggi's description and interpretation, what she believed Rob was arguing:

Rob was an English graduate who had then worked as a residential worker before deciding to train to be a qualified social worker. He argued that there was a credibility gap between, on the one hand, the theoretical model of problem-based learning, which was presented to the researchers in the initial stages of the course and the role tutors played within that theoretical model, and, on the other, the realities of their practice as tutors, facilitators and possibly even as social workers. Rob believed that even though tutors spoke of wanting to devolve power to the researchers, that in practice they were either not prepared to or not capable of doing so. He explained:

Quotation that she believes represents his perspective and her interpretation

to my mind it feels there is an element of hanging on to power because to devolve it to the researchers is like we're baiting them kind of. It's a bit like residential workers saying to kids 'Who are you to know?' The chances are they know very well how it feels like and what they need to grow and develop and move on ... The academic staff have certain things they need to ensure happen, but there feels to me as a researcher an assumption 'we know and they don't' what is best for us and that's the bit that makes me feel – I sometimes wonder whether we are mature researchers or not. I'm 36 years of age, I've been working in the social work field for 10 years, I feel like I've some experience and some knowledge and yet that doesn't feel valued in terms of how I use it here or any changes that are made. It's almost as if I have no voice in that.

Her reflection in the interpretation and a further interpretation of the issues for Rob in the broader context of his relationship with staff and researchers

Not feeling valued and not being heard on a course that he initially believed promoted collaboration and valued prior experience was a huge contradiction. Rob challenged this contradiction. Learning for Rob was seen as an area of commonality where staff–researcher and researcher–researcher relationships were central to an individual's personal stance. His ability to ground his learning in the context of his lived experience and to know the world differently was dependent upon the personal stances of the staff and researchers with whom he worked and learned.

Here we see how my values about Rob and his position resulted in this particular interpretation. In this example as a researcher you see me siding with Rob because I felt students needed to have their voices heard. Staff, I assumed, were patronising students and students were voiceless in the face of powerful staff. Later reflections show that in many areas of this research I tended to side with the students because of my then belief in student empowerment – at any price – a view modified as I researched staff perspectives in problem-based learning.

Thus the actual process of the interpretation is difficult to express in a transparent way. It is difficult in some senses to define what mental processes are required for interpretation.

We believe that the concept of epiphany has something of value to offer in considering how the process of interpretation occurs. The term epiphany derives from the Greek word, epiphainein, meaning 'to manifest'. The concept of epiphany has several interesting connotations. In a religious context, it is a Christian holiday, marked by the visit of the wise men to Jesus shortly after his birth; the notion of revelation is important in this sense. The term has several literary associations and among the most prominent writers to rely upon it as a literary device arguably were James Joyce, who used it to highlight important moments, and Flannery O'Connor, whose characters often experienced an epiphany when challenged by a dark event or character; again, revelation is key.

In the context of interpretative research, epiphanies also have interesting connotations, as illustrated by Denzin (1989). Denzin describes the personal epiphanies that respondents go through in relating their experiences. A personal epiphany, he suggests, is an 'interactional moment' which occurs when a challenge or set of challenges result in a crisis or change to someone's meaning perspective. Denzin proposed four different types of epiphany that respondents go through that can create such change.

- Major: important moments of truth or turning points.
- Cumulative: a series of events that leads to revelation.
- Illustrative: a point in time or particular experience that reveals insights; or an event that raises issues that are problematic.
- Relived: an event or issue that has to be relived in order to be understood.

While the first two epiphanies are sparked by an event, the last two are of particular use in thinking about the process of interpretation. Drawing from these ideas, then, we believe that these various accounts of how a revelation or illumination occurs also can inform our thinking about the process a synthesist follows when reading and rereading, thinking and rethinking in order to come to understand text.

Developing third order interpretations

The shift from the second order theme to third level interpretation is complex. The process involves reviewing important patterns and connections among first and second order themes and ensuring that iterative cycles of interpretation occur. In practice this means that not only are data compared and condensed across the studies but so are themes, metaphors, ideas, concepts and contexts are revisited and rethought. Third order themes, then, emerge from interactive interpretation. In theory, the process may be envisioned as follows:

Theme 1 =>
Theme 2 =>   Composite theme=>
Theme 3 =>

Theme 4 =>
Theme 5 =>   Composite theme=>   Interpretation
Theme 6 =>
Theme 7 =>

Theme 8 =>   Composite theme=>
Theme 9 =>

It is important to note, however, that we believe that a danger exists, even in early stages of interpretation, to oversimplify and to develop bland categories that are a 'catchall' for most of the themes that people raise in the studies used. By listing themes we can be tempted to fit what people said to these, rather than actually letting complexity emerge. What happens to many synthesists when attempting interpretation is that data can seem disparate and unconnected, and then there becomes a huge reluctance to let go of initial categories because somehow they seem safe and logical. At this stage then it is important to move away from broad themes, such as 'learning' or 'assessment,' or trying to identify the common meanings in these categories across all data. Instead it is important to explore organizing principles, which in the example of the theme of 'learning and assessment' would explore how notions of learning and assessment are used by different participants, in different contexts, to argue a point or take up a particular stance. Further, third order interpretations often emerge from subthemes that reveal a subtext that is not apparent in the initial common themes. The process also requires trans-study interpretation and the location of the researchers themselves in a broader cultural interpretation which is both in-depth and situated.

As we noted above, the process of interpretation can be difficult to capture and express. We believe what may be expressed, however, is the product of the process. The presentation of the emergence of interpretation from first order analysis and second order comparison, for example, may be presented as follows:

Table 4.6 Developing third order interpretations (from Savin-Baden et al., 2008)

Overarching themes	Second order interpretations	Third order interpretations
Practice	Improving practice Changing practice The impact of innovation Creation of theory Understanding students Staff experiences	Identity Agency Disjunction Academic stances Notions of improvement Learning spaces Academic cultures Communities of practice
Community	Disciplinary communities Online/e-learning communities Education development communities Inquiry-based learning communities	
Transfer	Transfer for shared practice Transfer related to policy	

From Savin-Baden, M., Macfarlane, L. and Savin-Baden, J. (2008) 'Learning spaces, agency and notions of improvement: Influencing thinking and practices about teaching and learning in higher education. An interpretive meta-ethnography', *London Review of Education*, 6(3): 211–229. Routledge Taylor & Francis Ltd. http://www.informaworld.com/, reprinted with permission of the publisher.

What we see in this table is the move toward an interpretive position and thus the product of the process is demonstrated in a transparent way. Such a depiction of the product allows the researcher sufficient information to make inferences about the processes that took place.

Allowing movement

As we have indicated, findings from the original studies will not all fit neatly in second order themes or third order interpretations. We believe that it is critical to not only allow for difference but also highlight it when it occurs. Unlike some who have argued that it is important to preserve structure of relationships between concepts (for example Britten *et al.*, 2002; Malpass *et al.*, 2009), we argued in one of our qualitative syntheses that such preservation was not necessary and indeed that 'Because we believed that forcing all data into common themes results in questionable research practices, though, we retained issues that diverged, pointing out differences' (Savin-Baden and Major, 2007: 84–2).

We further believe it is important to explain difference, when it is possible to do so. Indeed, 'fittingness' only is considered reached when findings apply to other contexts and reflect both typical *and* atypical elements of the situation (Jensen and Allen, 1996; Bondas and Hall, 2007). We should also note, following Noblit and Hare (1988), that we believe that a real synthesis allows for the possibility of failure. In other words, the comparison, metaphor or analogy ultimately may break down and reveal that studies are not compatible; while studies may appear similar on the surface, they may have substantive differences that make them irreconcilable.

Reflecting upon the processes and products

During the process of synthesis, we believe it important to consider the issue of ownership so there is a sense that what we eventually present are shared truths and shared values so that peoples' norms and values, including our own, are always evident. We believe this because it seems unacceptable to us to talk about collaborative inquiry when there is no evidence of collaboration; to advocate client-centred practice but leave the client voiceless in the reporting of the study; and to lay claim to an interpretive study but show no evidence of interpretation or, if this is done, not share those interpretations with participants. Thus throughout the process of analysis and synthesis, leading to interpretation, we need to ask ourselves questions. We offer the question set in Table 4.7 as a guide.

Thoughts on using technology for data management and synthesis

Several software packages exist that can help manage data for qualitative synthesis. Some of those packages that have a long history of use with primary

Table 4.7 Transparency questions

Level 1 Analysis	Which findings are clear?
	Which articles contain which themes?
	What themes diverge amongst the articles?
Level 2 Synthesis	What is the level of discomfort that discrepancies cause the synthesist?
	Has the synthesist allowed for the possibility of failure?
Level 3 Interpretation	Which data are privileged and which are not?
	Whose voices proliferate?
	How are data managed, interpreted and presented and who decides?
	What possible explanations might be offered for what seem to be contradictions?

qualitative research, such as NUD*IST (now called N6) allow for indexing and searching (Pope *et al.*, 2007) which could be of use in a qualitative research synthesis. Nvivo7 allows for coding, retrieval and data connection, which also has potential application for synthesis of qualitative evidence. Dixon-Woods *et al.* (2006) demonstrated the use of such software in their meta-synthesis of 119 papers. The Joanna Briggs Institute also has software for managing a meta-synthesis. The Qualitative Assessment and Review Instrument (JBI-QARI) allows for handling of large data sets of qualitative data as a part of a systematic review. This Web-based software allows for data management, extraction, appraisal, synthesis, and reporting (Pope *et al.*, 2007).

While many use these products with good results, it is important for us to acknowledge that we find that to truly engage with the data and let themes emerge and develop in a reflexive cycle, it is critical to have some 'hands on' work with the data set. Hands on data analysis, synthesis, and interpretation helps to avoid oversimplification during synthesis and interpretation that can be compounded by the use of computer packages that tend to break things down into detailed themes and words that result in deconstruction rather than reconstruction of the data. We both tend to undertake the processes of analysis, synthesis, and interpretation by hand.

Conclusion

It is quite common for a synthesis to contain thick description of the search and selection process. It also is common for it to include a description of the various levels of synthesis, which generally involves a description of first, second and third order interpretations. It is much rarer, however, for a synthesist to describe what has actually been *done* to the data during the processes of analysis and interpretation. Perhaps such omissions occur because many synthesists believe

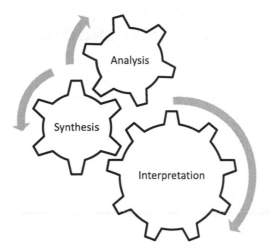

Figure 4.2 The iterative cycle of qualitative research synthesis.

that standard qualitative techniques are implied; alternatively it might be because of the fact that at some point it is difficult to describe the inferential processes involved.

We have argued in this chapter that the process of synthesis involves three levels: analysis, synthesis and interpretation of data, and suggested that it is the synthesists's job to be as transparent as possible at about the process. We recognize, however, that at some levels, establishing transparency of these levels is nearly impossible. In some cases, synthesists can make the products of the processes tangible and transparent. Doing so will provide the reader with sufficient information to make inferences about the processes and thus make informed judgments about the rigour of the study and plausibility of the findings.

While we outlined the process in a linear way to describe the various events that occur at different levels, we have argued contrastingly that it may be best to conceive of it as an iterative and interlocking cycle. This cycle may be depicted in Figure 4.2.

It is only when synthesists can truly view the process as cyclical and iterative that the meaning from the original studies can emerge and present itself. It is critical for synthesists to articulate the cycle as doing so can lead to greater levels of transparency, which we examine in Chapter 5.

Establishing plausibility in qualitative research synthesis

In this chapter, we acknowledge that there are many practical challenges for ensuring that studies using qualitative synthesis are rigorous and that the findings are plausible. Many of these difficulties are inherent in qualitative methods generally and thus can be exacerbated in qualitative synthesis of these studies. Many of them are unique to the process of synthesis. In this chapter, therefore, we attempt to offer suggestions for establishing the plausibility of a qualitative research synthesis. We begin the chapter by describing some of the common misconceptions about how credibility may be established in syntheses. We then describe our ideas for ensuring rigour and following plausibility, which we necessarily previewed in Chapters 3 and 4 as we described the processes of synthesis. Here, we elaborate on many of these concepts providing further details about then. We additionally provide a framework for thinking through the processes. Furthermore, we outline concrete ideas and suggestions for how the framework may be applied in the practice of synthesis.

Common misconceptions about establishing plausibility in qualitative synthesis

As might be expected, because qualitative synthesis is a complex and relatively new approach to analysing and interpreting qualitative studies, establishing plausibility can be problematic. Synthesists can make many mistakes in the process of ensuring rigour that invariably cause difficulties that could have been avoided. In this section, we describe some of these misconceptions and the challenges that they present.

Plausibility is easy and straight forward to ensure in syntheses

There often is a sense that it is easy to ensure plausibility in qualitative synthesis. The assumption is based on the idea that because the research activity centres on data extraction and collation of existing studies, plausibility will occur naturally because the articles included have a built-in validity factor, particularly since they have been peer reviewed and published. Yet many articles do not include transparent explanations of validity, leaving the researcher wondering whether efforts to ensure validity have been followed, and if so how. Similarly, perhaps because it is believed to be built-in, few synthesists address efforts toward validity or other approaches to ensure rigour and thus plausibility in their own work. If qualitative synthesis is to advance as an approach, we must be rigorous not only in evaluating original studies, but also in developing and documenting our own methods and evaluative processes.

Most published qualitative articles will meet baseline quality criteria

When developing inclusion and exclusion criteria which are usually quite broad, it is easy to assume that many, if not most, of the studies identified preliminarily will meet them. Such an assumption can cause synthesists to lower their guards against poorly designed and articulated research. However, it is rarely the case that all articles will meet the quality criteria. Articles may be fatally flawed, or at least lack adequacy of description to ensure that they are not, which necessarily disqualifies them from inclusion. Synthesists often uncover articles that appear at face value to meet the criteria, only to discover that

a methodology is not explicit;
b data are absent from presentation;
c data presentation lacks thick description that can be analysed;
d studies that argued they were qualitative were in fact mixed methods;
e studies which suggested they were qualitative turned interview data into descriptive, or statistics;
f studies were published many years after data were collected.

Synthesists should strive to be vigilant in their application of quality criteria to ensure the rigour of a synthesis, as well as to document these efforts to do so, as we described in Chapter 4.

Studies are always methodologically located

One of the most common difficulties synthesists encounter is that, having decided to include studies that were qualitative in design and which relied on interviews, focus groups, online discussions or observations, many of those studies identified are not methodologically positioned. For example, the authors might argue that the overarching methodology adopted is narrative inquiry. Yet the following description of methods they provide is thin; thus, there is no way to tell whether they used narrative inquiry or some other qualitative approach. Alternatively, often the authors do not describe a conceptual framework so there is little relationship between the methodology adopted and the way data were managed and interpreted. Synthesists should strive to select and include articles within the same methodological tradition if not the same method, as we described in Chapter 3 in our consideration of inclusion and exclusion criteria, to ensure the rigour of the synthesis as well as to establish a firm methodological base for the designs and approaches adopted.

There is clarity about how data were managed and interpreted

When exploring different primary studies it is often, but not always, possible to locate information about how data were collected and managed in the description presented in the articles. Yet studies often are missing in accounts of how data were interpreted. Frequently, then, it is difficult to see how shifts were made between analysis and interpretation. Qualitative synthesis requires situating studies against each other and determining where differences exist. Synthesists should strive to use articles that had similar approaches to collection and management. Furthermore, synthesists should strive for transparent processes that demonstrate clearly translations of study themes and categories into others, the kind for which we advocated in Chapter 4.

Traditional tests for validity and trustworthiness are easily applied to qualitative synthesis

In our own work we have been challenged by reviewers to consider difficulties with validity as they relate to qualitative synthesis. 'Validity' as a term in qualitative research has been increasingly replaced by 'trustworthiness', because the latter is seen as a term that provides a more transparent representation of the ways in which the qualitative researcher seeks to ensure credibility in the research process. The difficulty with validity as a concept, and an approach, is that it is inherently about truth claims. For something to be deemed valid or validated, it is seen to be grounded in some sort of truth; for something to be trustworthy largely relies on a 'Trust me, I'm a good researcher' mentality. Even so, the practices and processes associated with validity and trustworthiness (or another way to ensure plausibility) often are not made explicit or even presented in many qualitative studies and in even fewer syntheses.

When synthesists make efforts to demonstrate validity or trustworthiness, they often fall back on the practices advocated in primary qualitative research, particularly on the notions of credibility, transferability, dependability and confirmability (initially outlined by Lincoln and Guba, 1985). The fact that these conceptions are relied upon more than 30 years after their development is a testimony to the need to document credibility in qualitative research, as well as to the usefulness of various aspects and suggestions of their approaches. Yet we see particular challenges for the application of many traditional notions of validity and trustworthiness to syntheses. While synthesis shares some common features with primary qualitative research, it is a different process, and so applying these approaches designed for another kind of research must be approached with caution. We discuss these concerns further in the following sections.

Credibility

The term credibility is centred on the idea that results are credible and therefore to be believed. It is the idea that the reader can have confidence in the data and their interpretation. The term credibility is the qualitative parallel to the positivist notion of internal validity, the idea that the findings describe some level of reality. The underlying notion is there is a central 'truth' to data that should be examined. The ideas behind credibility are thus somewhat misplaced in qualitative syntheses, since there is an inherent positivist assumption in the intimation that there are 'known points' or positions from which it is possible to compare methods, data and researcher stances with relative ease, even while acknowledging that there are multiple realities. In the application of the notion of credibility to qualitative synthesis, the expectation exists to establish credibility, or truth, of a combination of multiple studies.

Transferability

Transferability refers to the idea that findings may be applicable in similar situations. While transferability generally is considered the responsibility of the one who wishes to apply the results into new contexts, the researcher generally is expected to have provided sufficient information about context and assumptions to determine whether the research is transferrable. Transferability too in some ways is a positivist overlay on a qualitative process, developed out of the notion of generalizability, or the idea that findings will be stable across multiple settings. Transferability resists the urge to say that qualitative findings will hold up in different contexts, but indicates that there may be degrees of similarity between the findings if another setting or context is comparable.

Synthesists often are expected to demonstrate transferability. They often believe that they have done so by design, as they have combined studies from multiple sites and contexts. Yet the synthesis often depends upon combining studies with similar context, which may or may not have applicability elsewhere. It is critical to articulate the boundaries of the synthesis in order to establish what it does and does not intend to do.

Dependability

Dependability is the notion that the research can be trusted over time. Dependability is derived from the more positivist perspectives of reliability and replicability. These ideas still underpin the naturalistic description of dependability, which requires the researcher to thoroughly document the context in which the research has been undertaken. Synthesists often are expected to document dependability, yet often context is sufficiently, but not elaborately, described in the original studies.

Confirmability

Confirmability is in some senses the idea that the researcher has remained neutral in data analysis and interpretation. It is based upon the notion that the researcher needs to demonstrate that results could be and at times even should be confirmed or corroborated by others. Yet this concept can belie the interpretive nature necessary for synthesis, particularly when taken together with standard procedures to demonstrate confirmability, such as inter-rater reliability upon which many reviewers insist, which may not be the best way to ensure that the researcher has controlled against bias (Table 5.1).

Table 5.1 Summary of the ways in which common challenges with qualitative research are exacerbated in qualitative synthesis

Category of concern	Application to primary studies	Application to synthesis
Validity is easy to establish	Need to examine and account for it	Need to describe
Articles meet baseline quality	Need to establish criteria and be vigilant in ensuring included studies meet it	Need to hold synthesis accountable for the same, and articulate how this was done
Studies are methodologically located	Need to review not only terminology but also descriptions of processes, if available	Need to hold synthesis to the same standard of locating a methodologically grounded approach to synthesis
Methods of data management and interpretation are clear	Need to review primary studies for clarity	Need to ensure clarity and transparency of the synthesis
Traditional notions of validity are evident and appropriate	Need to ensure that primary studies have set some criteria for establishing credibility and have followed them	Need to be consistent in the application of a set of criteria, techniques and processes appropriate for synthesis

Frequently used techniques for establishing validity

In primary qualitative research, there is an ever growing toolkit of techniques for establishing validity or trustworthiness. While some of these approaches are useful in synthesis research, and indeed we have used some of them ourselves within our own framework, it is important for a synthesist to approach them with care, because there are inherent challenges in using them for qualitative synthesis. In Table 5.2 we outline some of the most frequently used tools as well as their attending challenges, when applied to syntheses.

Table 5.2 Description of commonly used strategies for validity and attending cautions

Strategy	Description	Application	Caution
Conceptual framing	Using an existing theory to guide study design and interpretations	Adopting a conceptual or theoretical frame in one or more of the original studies or selecting a new one to guide interpretations	If synthesists rely upon a framework too heavily it can lock them into a predetermined idea of what the data 'should' be
Dense description of context	Providing sufficient information about the culture and context within which the research is situated, so that readers can ascertain whether the findings would be the same in similar contexts	Elaborate description of studies included in review, comparing contexts	Relying too heavily on context in original studies, rather than viewing them as a unified data set, can lead the synthesist to make inferences that may or may not be accurate
Dense description of findings	The synthesist presents a sufficient number of strings of data so the reader may judge whether the research is transferable	Detailed quotations from the original studies	Relying too heavily on thick description can lead to laziness on the part of the synthesist, who may not be doing due diligence in interpretation. Furthermore, most dissemination outlets have space and word count limitations that can prevent dense sampling of primary data
Dense description of methods	The researcher describes various approaches that original researchers have employed to make clear whether the findings are transferrable	Explicit description of methods, from searching strategies, inclusion and exclusion criteria, to data analysis and interpretations	Often the original studies have short-handed methods sections and have used imprecise terminology. In describing their approach to synthesis in detail, synthesists risk having their work turned into 'methods' paper, with an attending short shrift to results

Continued

Table 5.2 Cont'd

Strategy	Description	Application	Caution
Experience over time	Selecting studies to seek a longitudinal review	Using studies that were written within a given timeframe	Dramatic events can cause changes that will affect data even within a narrow timeframe
Member checking	Through checking with participants for feedback or verification of interpretation, research is thought to be more credible	Contacting authors of original studies to ensure interpretations are retained	Since they have not read the other studies, authors may see things differently from the synthesist. Authors thus may argue that the interpretation is incorrect; often this occurrence can change a synthesist's perspective, whether rightly or wrongly, and thus can negatively affect data transformation
Peer examination	Having peers review various phases of the research to confirm suitability	Multiple authors each reviewing and coding articles; using multiple raters to establish interrater reliability	Often qualitative synthesists are expected to prove inter-rater reliability. This is a positivist perspective that threatens the interpretive nature of the undertaking
Researcher positionality statement	Spending time establishing the synthesist's role in the process	Explicitly stating synthesist's qualifications; acknowledging stance and potential for bias	Due to the inherent nature of the interpretive process, there is a sense that what is being sought is not a stance against bias, but a view that the research process will enable a 'better set' of biases to be created – which occurs through a deeper understanding of the issue under study

Table 5.2 Cont'd

Strategy	Description	Application	Caution
Triangulation	Through triangulation or cross examination at multiple points, the idea is that the research is more credible. Triangulation may be of data (time, space and persons), investigators (multiple researchers), theory (more than one scheme applied), or method (using more than one method) (Denzin, 1978)	Inclusion of studies that rely upon different methods, samples, contexts, etc	Triangulation tends to encourage the cleaning up of data, tidying data into themes and ignoring those data which do not fit. There is an assumption that data, people, contexts and methods can be triangulated and that taking up such an approach will necessarily result into some kind of quality validity. But as we noted above, this is rarely the case in syntheses

Critical conceptions for evaluating plausibility in qualitative research synthesis

In this section, we describe conceptions of plausibility that we believe are particularly appropriate for qualitative syntheses. We argue for several approaches; while not new to qualitative research generally, since these concepts are discussed infrequently in texts and articles about qualitative synthesis, they offer a unique way for framing the quest for plausibility in syntheses and thus are worthy of additional attention here. Please see Figure 5.1 overleaf.

Locating 'realities'

The notion of whether truth exists and whether it can be ascertained is one that has been discussed and debated *ad nauseum*. Notions of 'Truth', 'truth', 'truths', 'truthfulness', and even 'truthiness' have been considered for their applicability in social science research. While these concepts clearly are value laden and may be picked apart for accuracy, precision, desirability and achievability it is still clear that the researcher should make some effort to establish a semblance of confidence in the accurate treatment and interpretation of data to present some version at least of multiple realities. This is no less true for synthesis, and in fact, it may be argued that the bar is even higher for ensuring that synthesists have

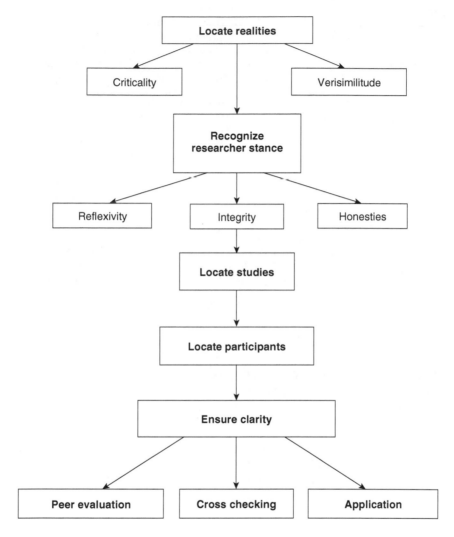

Figure 5.1 Designing for plausibility.

done their best to create an accurate representation of the experiences of large numbers of participants in multiple studies. We believe that two concepts can help synthesists think about these issues: verisimilitude and criticality.

Verisimilitude

As noted earlier in this chapter, the notion of credibility is linked to the concept that a central truth exists that may be uncovered. Verisimilitude, although an unwieldy term, is simple in that it argues for demonstrating the appearance of truth; the quality of seeming to be true, which is arguably a more realistic quest than uncovering 'truth'. The underlying idea is that research cannot prove anything true; rather, research could focus on disproving truth. By disproving more and more truths, the researcher then comes closer to discovering truths, by a study of what has been disproven. The concept of verisimilitude thus can be used as a vehicle through which an analysis framework may be scrutinized and findings examined in more depth.

Denzin, in fact, proposed deconstructive verisimilitude as a strategy that might be used to provide legitimate answers to the research questions. This strategy is accomplished through interrogation of that which 'seems to be true', considering conditions under which it might not be true or that which 'seems not to be true' that might indeed be true. He uses the analogy of a murder mystery novel to illustrate the use of verisimilitude as a standard of truth. He explained that what seems to be true in such novels is usually shown to be untrue, while what seems untrue is often found to be true (Denzin, 1989).

The outcomes of questioning verisimilitude are provisional. Thus, such considerations provide a rich foundation for further interpretation. These considerations can be particularly useful in the shift for moving from synthesis of data to interpretations, as well as for allowing for cross checking of central concepts.

Criticality

In Chapter 2, in proposing that various approaches to the use of research literature fall along a continuum of complexity, we described 'criticality' as 'the behaviour of those who are engaged in the various phases on the scale [of using literature] and the complex cognitive functions that they must perform to complete each phase'. Here, we further note that the concept of criticality is related to verisimilitude and is the idea that researchers should strive for critical analysis and awareness while conducting and reviewing research. In conceptions of criticality too, scholars have indicated the need to position findings in ways that negations are sought, rather than affirmation of truth. In discussing criticality, Marshall (1990), for example, indicated the need to search for alternative hypotheses and negative instances, and to examine biases.

Locating the researcher and identifying stance

The position, stance and influence of the researcher also have received considered attention in social science research. The stance of the researcher is about how we position ourselves in relation to the methodology, participants and methods. It also relates to how we manage and construct data analysis and interpretation. Researcher stance is important as it helps us to see not only the (relative) plausibility, but also to see whether there is honesty and consistency between methods and researcher. Further, several issues hinge on researcher stance, which we have addressed previously, including potential problems with data retrieval, bias in sampling, researcher bias as well as scanty analysis, deductive contamination from theories and possible exaggeration of interpretations (Jensen and Allen, 1996; Major, 2010). In addition to the primary criteria concerning the stance of the researcher that we identified above, we believe that there are three concepts critical to locating the researcher within a synthesis: reflexivity, honesties, and integrity.

Reflexivity

Although many researchers argue for a reflexive design in qualitative research (see for example Whittemore *et al.*, 2001; Mays *et al.*, 2005) achieving reflexivity is a challenging task. Reflexivity, as Nightingale and Cromby (1999: 228) suggest:

> requires an awareness of the researcher's contribution to the construction of meanings throughout the research process, and an acknowledgment of the impossibility of remaining 'outside of' one's subject matter while conducting research. Reflexivity then, urges us 'to explore the ways in which a researcher's involvement with a particular study influences, acts upon and informs such research'.

Willig (2001) identifies two types of reflexivity, personal and epistemological. Personal reflexivity is a process in which researcher values, experiences and beliefs shape the research (p. 10). Not only is a consideration of how the researcher has shaped the research important, however, but also a consideration of how the research has in turn shaped the researcher is critical. Epistemological reflexivity involves exploring how the researcher's belief system has shaped research design as well as the interpretation of findings. These types of reflexivity clearly are related to the notion of a self-conscious design, for which we advocated in Chapter 3.

Reflexivity in qualitative synthesis therefore means seeking to continually challenge our biases and examining our stances, perspectives, and views as a researcher. This is not meant to be a notion of 'situating oneself' as formulaic as pronouncing a particular positioned identity connected with class, gender or race for example, but rather situating oneself in order to interpret data demands so to engage with critical questions. We hope that in Chapters 3 and 4 we provided sound guidance on how to accomplish this through reflection and questioning processes.

Honesties

Honesties (following Stronach *et al.*, 2002) as a concept allows us to acknowledge not only the cyclical nature of 'truths', but also that the nature of honesties is defined by people and contexts and also helps us to avoid the prejudice *for* similarity and *against* difference in data interpretation. Furthermore, data about ethics, conduct and accountability can be distinguished by differences of theory and practical action, but they can never actually be isolated from one another. Issues such as these in both research and practice demand that we engage with deceptions – our own and those involved in the research – and this in turn forces us to consider how we deal with such (benevolent) deception. For example, studies that focus on outcomes at the expense of process do little justice to participants and their lives.

We believe there are a number of ways that we can engage with honesties in the research process and we believe four in particular are important for the synthesis, as identified by Savin-Baden and Fisher (2002):

1   situating ourselves in relation to participants;
2   voicing mistakes;
3   situating ourselves in relation to the data;
4   taking a critical stance towards research.

Integrity

A notion related to reflexivity and honesties is researcher integrity. This idea identifies the researcher as a person who will necessarily enable a unique interpretation of a data set (Johnson, 1999). The researcher must strive, therefore, for integrity, which may best be accomplished by ensuring that interpretations are grounded within the data.

Situating ourselves in research is always a complex activity, partly because our perspectives change and move as we undertake the research, and partly because of the way we interpret data and make sense of people and their contexts. This kind of interpretation involves situating ourselves not just in the stages of the research, but also in relation to the data we analysed and interpreted in the studies. This may sound obvious, but too often we ignore our own stances and perspectives and act as if we are sitting outside the articles (and not acknowledging that we are interpreting and judging as we read). It is often easier to adopt complicated coding strategies than to engage with the messiness and complexity of reinterpreting data. Analysing them in a simplistic way just leaves lists of themes, thin description and little, if any, broader cultural interpretation.

Locating the included studies

This involves examining the way data have been analysed. For example, it is often possible to see the organizing principles, defined here as the categories used by people to justify, explain, defend and define their stance and the themes located. The ways in which people talk about themselves, how they define themselves, can help us to see their values, how they see themselves in relation to one another and in relation to the organization and profession. These issues should be considered for their relationship to the synthesists. It may be important for example for synthesists to consider how they could have organized and categorized differently, in order to consider how stance might be affecting view of the original studies.

Locating the participants

The fourth conceptual consideration for establishing credibility in qualitative synthesis is how participants can be located. The most critical concept for this discussion is the notion of authenticity. Authenticity is the notion that research should reflect the lived experiences of the participants. The researcher should exhibit an awareness of the difference in voices of participants, no matter how subtle (Lincoln, 1995). The notion is that multiple realities must be portrayed (Bailey, 1996). When examining an article, it is important to explore how people's perspectives of themselves and others shape the contexts in which they live. Thus, we suggest the need for more transparent and reflexive approaches that help us to engage with the way that participants in original studies often tell contradictory stories so that they are 'caught between stories, split between grounding narrative that offer(ed) different versions of a professional self along with tangential manifestations of a personal self' (Stronach et al., 2001: 16).

Using conceptions of clarity in analysis and interpretation

As researchers and practitioners, we have a duty not only to undertake and promote transparent research practices but also to critique the practices of others. Too often we assume that because research is published in high level journals or written by an eminent author – or at least someone we have heard of – the research is necessarily plausible and done well. Yet research is always flawed, and we need to question the extent to which the researchers have followed the methodology that they adopted right through to the data interpretation section. We need to examine whether the data really have been interpreted, and to ensure that the research not only has been rigorous but also has engaged with the multiplicity of truths and honesties that emerges from participants' stories. In addition, we need to hold ourselves accountable to the same standards.

Cross checking

We recommend using the following framework, illustrated in Table 5.3 for cross checking for location of realities, location of synthesist and location of participants.

Table 5.3 A framework for questioning whether four central criteria have been met

Primary criteria	Critical questions for the synthesist
Locating realities	What reality or truths are expressed in the primary studies that seem to be accepted without any scrutiny?
	Which experiences/opinions in the primary studies initially seem improbable; what conditions might show these to be real?
	What contradictions are revealed, could these be reconciled in any way?
	What strategies in synthesizing the studies will ensure critical reflection and critical thinking?
	How will you demonstrate that inquiry involved critical appraisal of key decisions? How are your interpretations grounded in data?
Locating the researcher	What strategies will ensure that the original researcher is located within the research? The synthesist?
	To what extent has the researcher in the primary studies influenced the research in the following ways:
	– Defining a research question that limits the articles that emerge? Designing a method of analysis that constructs data and findings?
	– The synthesist?
	What is being realized through the primary research, by whom, for whom? Through the synthesis?
	What are you arguing for in the interpretation of these data?
Locating the included studies	How might the primary studies be organized differently?
	How will the synthesist stay true to the original organizations and interpretations?
Locating the researched	What steps have been taken to ensure that participant voices are recognized in the synthesis in a believable way?
	How will multiple realities be represented?
	How are people's biographies being taken account of in the arguments of the text of the synthesis?
	How has an emic perspective been portrayed in the synthesis?

In addition to the primary criteria that we described in detail above, there are also several secondary criteria that synthesists can use to guide thinking as well. Explicitness is the notion that as synthesist, we should try to be as clear and demonstrative as possible, leaving as little as possible for inference. Vividness is that we try to present as animated a picture as possible of the phenomenon that we are studying. Creativity, often seemingly at odds with rigour, is the idea that as synthesists, we need to transcend traditional rules and patterns in order to think about things in new ways. Thoroughness indicates that we need to give attention to details. Congruence indicates that our interpretations need to agree with, or bear some resemblance to, what is presented in the original studies; our interpretations should not be contradictory. Sensitivity is the idea that we need to be tactful and to respect the participants and authors of the original studies. We outline questions that can help us follow these criteria in Table 5.4.

Table 5.4 A framework for questioning whether secondary criteria have been met

Secondary criteria	Critical questions for the synthesist
Explicitness	How do records document decisions and processes of the synthesis? How have the synthesist's biases been exposed?
Vividness	How have data been presented in rich and compelling description in the synthesis, without excessive detail?
Creativity	How has the creative process of synthesis allowed for the development of insightful interpretations? How are findings presented in an insightful and original way? How does the inquiry document a new perspective?
Thoroughness	How have sampling processes and data gathering in the synthesis ensured a relative degree of saturation? How has attention been paid to sampling, data saturation, conceptual completion and information richness in the synthesis?
Congruence	How have the processes ensured logical, philosophical, theoretical and methodological congruence in the synthesis?
Sensitivity	How has an ethical and sensitive respect for participants and contexts been reflected in the synthesis?

Peer evaluation

An additional step toward ensuring credibility can involve using peers in several phases of the process. Experts, colleagues, or members of the primary studies may examine codes and coding and review findings. Attention should also be given to what was not said, and to the prominence given to those aspects that were shared.

- What expressed reality or truths are expressed that seem to be accepted without any scrutiny?
- Which experiences/opinions initially seem improbable; what conditions might show these to be real?
- What contradictions are revealed? Under what conditions might these be reconciled?

Claire tells the story of how she used peer evaluation in one of her recent qualitative syntheses.

Because of the importance of retaining the interpretations of the researchers to synthesis methods, I believe that member checks are useful for qualitative synthesis methods. For this reason, I involved the authors of the original studies in member checking. I sent an email initially to the primary author of approximately half of the studies (four). I introduced myself, told them of my research and about the inclusion of their work in the study, and I asked for their assistance. I attached a full length working draft of the paper. I asked them in particular to provide comments on my findings and conclusions to indicate whether my interpretations were consistent with their findings, and to provide comments about the overall document as desired. I noted that my findings would not be the same as theirs because of the inclusion of additional studies, but asked whether they saw them as valid interpretations, or whether I needed correction/elaboration in any of the themes identified, implications highlighted, or conclusions drawn. All four authors responded. Their responses provided support and encouragement for the work and ranged in depth from surface corrections to ongoing conversations about the nature of the field of faculty experiences online and the nature of qualitative research. I revised the document based upon their responses. I then sent the revised paper to the lead or contact authors from the remaining five studies for review, with the same request for assistance. Four of five authors responded. Again they indicated support for the work. The authors offered points of clarification of their interpretations, which most often validated the interpretations. Occasionally the authors provided information that complemented and extended the interpretations, and these comments are indicated in the end notes. Their comments suggested additional conclusions, particularly those providing practical advice for institutions.

(Major, 2010)

Applications to policy and practice that are based on trustworthy interpretation

In many earlier qualitative syntheses, third level themes are presented as findings in a way that seem to expect readers to decide on the implications themselves. If qualitative synthesis is to be seen as valid and useful for informing policy and practice, it is vital that third level interpretations are presented with clear implications and where possible, with recommendations for policy and practice. It is vital that any claims made can be shown to have emerged through a transparent process of interpretation. It is also worth comparing the recommendations of the qualitative synthesis with those of the included studies.

Conclusion

In this chapter, we have asserted that it is critical to be as rigorous as possible to make the research process clear. The use of qualitative research synthesis also often implies that drawing up a set of rules for 'systematically' reviewing evidence will necessarily make the process of the review and research transparent. However, we have attempted to provide some concepts and guidelines that can help synthesists achieve a measure of plausibility. We further note that the way in which we present our findings can illustrate plausibility, and it is to this we turn in our final chapter, Chapter 6.

Presenting the synthesis

Introduction

The primary purpose of developing a synthesis is to aggregate and interpret findings from original studies for presentation in an easily accessible form. We argue that in presenting the synthesis, it is critical for synthesists to speak directly to a specific, intended audience. Further, we suggest that the selection of an intended audience is likely to drive decisions about how the synthesis is presented. In this chapter, we begin by discussing several issues related to the audience of the synthesis. We then delineate the way in which synthesists might write to a given audience throughout the various elements of reporting the synthesis.

Audience

As we have argued earlier in this book, in the past, researchers have undertaken the business of research for its own sake. While we still support and value this 'blue skies' research, because of the utilitarian turn that higher education has taken, we have noted that many researchers are now undertaking research for a particular purpose to encourage change and/or influence policy. Such a position introduces questions about who counts as the change agents. We assert that the answer depends upon the context. In the context of a university, for example, teachers themselves are the ones closest to changes in the classroom, so a synthesis of research investigating a given pedagogical approach may be of value to the teacher. Researchers often have a direct interest in the field and it may be argued that at a given point in time, the literature of the field *is* the field, so they may find a synthesis useful for a specific identification of ways that research can move in the future. A synthesis may also be of use to university leaders, who make decisions that directly affect the teaching process, such as how long a class period will last, where teaching and instructional development funds will be implemented, what teaching activities to encourage and support on campus (and which not to). Finally, such a report might be of great use to charities and government agencies who will determine how to direct funds to accomplish the greatest change, as broadly conceived.

As the audience can vary so greatly, it is critical to determine who the intended audience for the synthesis is at the outset. In stating this, we believe it critical to make a distinction between the *intended audience* who are the group of readers that synthesists specifically are targeting and the reader, who might be anyone who comes across the report and reads it for any number of purposes. Identifying and addressing the intended audience specifically is important for several reasons:

1   The intended audience is related directly to purpose of the study. In our example about the university above, if the intended audience is the teacher, then the purpose of the synthesis might be to determine how the pedagogy might be best implemented. If the intended audience is a policy maker, then the purpose of the study might be to determine how the pedagogy might produce different outcomes. While it is clear that either paper might be useful to both groups, each group will find one of the topics more useful than the other.

2   Membership of an intended audience will influence the kinds of information that should be presented to set the context of the study. Different audiences will have different levels of knowledge about a topic, as well as different preconceptions or misconceptions. How much time synthesists will have to spend establishing the information required to counter misconceptions and to lay the foundation necessary to understand the findings, is also determined by the intended audience.

3   Identifying the intended audience affects the way that findings are presented. Policy makers will want short and succinct as well as visually appealing overviews. While anyone ideally might want this, other audiences, such as teachers and researchers, might in the end prefer to have less of an overview but rather more detail to providing guidance for specific actions that they might then take in practice or research. Knowing the intended audience then can help synthesists streamline the presentation of the findings.

4   Being clear about the intended audience will affect the recommendations made. For example, very different recommendations are likely to be of interest to a university leader compared with a teacher. In our example, a leader might be much more concerned with knowing about how to affect change on campus, or how to conduct staff development workshops, while a teacher might appreciate tips for applying a pedagogical approach in the classroom.

5   Knowing the intended audience will necessarily affect the conclusions that synthesists draw from the findings. What synthesists say about the process, the findings and the future should be directed to the intended audience. Targeting a specific group can allow for clarity of focus as well as economy of language.

These are overarching reasons for being clear about the intended audience. In the next section of this chapter, we address the main elements for reporting the results of a synthesis and, in so doing, we make recommendations for considering the audience.

Presenting a qualitative synthesis

The social science research paper tends to follow a fairly standard format and a report of a qualitative research synthesis is no exception. The way in which a synthesist addresses the various sections, however, differs in some respects to the way that a researcher of a primary study would. In Table 6.1, we outline the main elements of a social science research paper as they apply to a synthesis.

Table 6.1 Elements of a social science research paper

Element	Description
Introduction	Outlines the need for the study, often indicating a need for change in policy and practice
Related literature	Describes the key literature related to the synthesis; rather than filling a gap as in traditional studies, here the researcher argues for the need for aggregation to bridge a gap to understanding
Methodology	Contains a description and justification of conducting a synthesis as well as a description of processes that we outline in Chapters 3 and 4, such as a description of techniques for article search and a selection, description of assessment of article fit and quality, and a description of data analysis
Findings	Presents findings of the synthesis and interpretation of multiple studies, generally done in both narrative and visual form.
Discussion	Translates knowledge into useful and consumable information for a specific audience, generally attempting to appeal to both researchers and decision makers. Often makes suggestions for practice as well as for future research
Conclusion	Briefly summarizes the key findings and highlights their relevance and argues for the importance of having undertaken the synthesis

In the following few sections, we highlight the purpose of including these various sections in a synthesis and we offer suggestions for ways in which synthesists might develop them as they target a specific audience.

The introduction

The introduction is intended not only to draw reader attention and interest but to serve as the reader's orientation to various elements of the synthesis. As such, the introduction is the first signal of the research questions or issues to be investigated. The introduction also lays critical groundwork to establish the reader's knowledge of the topic and important contextual considerations. Finally, the introduction establishes the question that is under investigation as well as indicates that a synthesis will be the method of investigation.

We believe that not only is it important to outline this initial information in the introduction but also it is important in the introduction for synthesists to acknowledge the reader, whether implicitly or explicitly, thereby helping to gain attention and support for the work. Synthesists should strive to address this audience directly as they work through the different elements of the introduction. To consider how synthesists might target a specific audience, we suggest the following questions be set, as shown in Table 6.2.

Table 6.2 Questions about targeting the audience in the introduction

The topic	What does the intended audience know about the topic?
	What does the audience need to know?
The context	What connections are it likely that the intended audience has to the context of the synthesis?
The method	How many syntheses has the intended audience likely encountered?
	What broad information does the audience need to know about syntheses?

The related literature section

The question of what to include in a literature review of a synthesis paper is an interesting one. After all, isn't a synthesis a type of review? While we have explained our position in Chapters 1 and 2 that qualitative research synthesis is not a literature review, it does draw from a pool of existing literature to develop a data set. Thus, it may feel to synthesists like the literature has been exhausted through this effort and that nothing remains to be 'reviewed.'

Clearly all literature will not fall neatly into a category that will meet the initial criteria for inclusion in the synthesis, however. While some synthesists eschew the literature review altogether, we believe that it is an essential component in establishing the context and argument for conducting the synthesis. Further, we find that the literature review is essential for developing a comprehensive picture of existing literature and for indicating how potential bridges across themes and concepts can and should be built by means of conducting a synthesis. We believe that there are three primary techniques for reviewing literature that synthesists can draw upon to help reach an intended audience, which we describe below.

Overview of quantitative literature

Often a literature review in a qualitative research synthesis can outline the quantitative research that has investigated the same or similar topic. The quantitative literature related to a specific topic often is a good start because it generally addresses different questions than will appear in the qualitative literature. In this way, the literature review section can set the context or offer a point of comparison or contrast which can further add to the discussion section. For example, in Major's study (2010), the literature review outlined the quantitative literature of staff perceptions of distance education, which tends to focus on attitudes toward distance learning or on perceptions of benefits or challenges. Her synthesis examined staff experiences in online distance education, which often focused on changes they made to their personas, the structure and their relationships with students. In the conclusion, she was able to demonstrate where the literature bases overlapped and how the qualitative studies in many ways extended and explained some of the quantitative findings.

Furthermore, many meta-analytic articles have been conducted that may serve as a useful starting point. As we have noted, these generally begin with different questions than a qualitative synthesis and thus can provide useful contextual information about the topic under investigation. Such studies often have been read and cited by many and thus can be a good way to engage an intended audience around a common reading.

Provision of orienting concepts

One approach to using literature in a qualitative research synthesis is to overview or highlight the chief bodies of knowledge that the audience should understand, in order to be able to consume and appreciate the findings and interpretations at hand. This works particularly well when the research is not well known, or when it is doubtful that the audience has had much access or exposure to it. In Savin-Baden and Major (2007) for example, the synthesis was about how using problem-based learning changed staff teaching knowledge and practice. For their literature review, the authors provided an overview of four key areas of literature: teacher knowledge, pedagogical content knowledge/discipline-based pedagogy and staff experience of problem-based learning. Without information about these framing concepts, audience members who were unfamiliar with the knowledge bases would have had more difficulty understanding what staff may know about teaching and learning and thus how staff knowledge may change with time and experience.

The outline of a conceptual frame for interpretation

In addition to the above methods, a review of relevant literature can also be a useful strategy for describing a conceptual or theoretical framework that will guide the methodology as well as the discussion and conclusion. Unfortunately, the notion of having some kind of conceptual framework seems to have become lost or overlooked. Recent research into conceptual frameworks, for example, indicated that many PhD candidates struggle with the idea of conceptual frameworks.

> Their difficulty arose despite the sessions/tutorials that many had previously received elsewhere 'on research' ... The majority of candidates could identify concepts and relate them to their intended research design and research process. However, despite clarifying research questions and 'reading around-their-subject', one-third of candidates still had problems in visualising concepts within a framework.
>
> (Leshem and Trafford, 2007: 93)

Such difficulty might suggest that the lack of understanding or use of conceptual frameworks is having a long term impact on the quality of qualitative studies in general.

Of particular interest to those planning a synthesis, though, is that few have used theory in this kind of work (Morse, 2001). The argument is that the methodology should serve as the theoretical frame for the analysis and interpretation of data; some have even argued that synthesis (see Noblit and Hare, for example) should rely upon grounded theory for analysis and thus the themes should arise from the data rather than be viewed through the lens of theory.

On occasion a conceptual or theoretical framework has been used to guide interpretations. In Major's study referenced above, for example, she used Zuboff's classic text on how technology affects work by being either 'automating' or 'informating'. She also noted how this theory had been extended (Cooper, 2002) by others, who suggest that technology fundamentally alters relationships and perceptions of abstract categories such as time and space. These theories guided her interpretations, giving them a structural coherence. Thus if done well, using a conceptual or theoretical framework can help to ensure the rigour of the synthesis as to convey a sense of the researcher's frame of reference to audience members.

The methodology section

The methodology section serves several purposes. It involves presenting the argument for conducting a synthesis. It also outlines the specific steps that the synthesist took throughout the research process. Its overarching goal is to make the synthesis process transparent to the intended audience.

In particular, because qualitative synthesis is a relatively new process, it is critical to spend time describing the methods used. We recommend including descriptions of several sections that we outline in the table below, but we argue for keeping the descriptions clear and concise so that they are accessible for the intended audience. We also refer to other sections of this book where we have outlined the processes more fully. Please see Table 6.3.

We recommend that the text synthesists present may contain general overviews and a few charts to demonstrate methods clearly and concisely. For clarity, however, we recommend that more lengthy descriptions and complex tables or graphs are better located in an appendix.

Table 6.3 Useful sections to present for a qualitative synthesis

Section	Description	More information may be found in
Justification of research design	An overt argument for the choice of synthesis methods	Chapter 2
Article search and selection	A description of various processes involved in the research design and sample selection. Often this includes search protocols, the initial sample, inclusion and exclusion criteria and a description of article appraisal	Chapter 3
Description of data set	A narrative description of the articles selected as well as a tabular comparison of studies	Chapter 4
Description of data handling and analysis	The process for data analysis, interpretation and synthesis. A description of how documents were handled, how findings were extracted and how themes were developed	Chapter 4

The findings

The purpose of the findings section is to provide an opportunity to present what has been discovered through the process of synthesis. At the heart of the findings section, we believe, should be a narrative of the discoveries made. A narrative at its most fundamental level is a story or an account, whether real or fictional, that depicts events or experiences. The narrative, then, is synthesists' opportunity to tell the story that they found contained in the data. Synthesists must construct a plausible and compelling narrative of the topic under investigation. This stage presents an interesting challenge to synthesists, who do not have access to the participant's narrative; rather, they have access to the primary researcher's narrative. The development of a narrative for a synthesis, then, is twice removed from the source. This removal stands amidst the growing concern amongst qualitative researchers about the 'crisis of representation'. The idea here is that no human can adequately convey the experiences of another let alone a group of others. Scholars who use synthesis approaches have noted that this crisis is even intensified in synthesis research. The intensification occurs not only by how far removed synthesists are from the original source, but also through the lack of thought given to the difference between reality and representation (Sandelowski, 2006).

However, because of the many benefits that we outline in Chapter 1, synthesists finds themselves in the unique position of undertaking this daunting task. The overarching goal is to tell the story of the multiple presenters and authors directly and plausibly to the audience, recognizing that the story is indeed that: a story that represents the multiple realities of the participants. The process of telling this story, while being further removed from the original narrative, is similar to that which is undertaken in primary qualitative research. The process, then, involves constructing a logical narrative designed to weave the information together in a way that makes sense and that is plausible to the audience. Synthesists present the narrative by plotting themes in a logical order, presenting exemplars, and indicating the transitions. We believe it is possible to accomplish these goals by choosing a logical structure, relying on thick description, and using visual displays, which we discuss in the next few sections.

Selecting an organizational structure

The findings sections of qualitative research studies may take a number of forms and qualitative research synthesis is no exception to this rule. While we do not wish to prescribe any one structure, we believe that there are a few approaches to organization that can be particularly helpful in organizing a qualitative research synthesis. These are as follows:

1   Narrative logic: The idea behind a narrative ordering of a synthesis is that there is an overarching story implicit in the original studies that should be told. This story is unfolded and presented with an eye toward the artistic and creative elements of story-telling. Chronology often is the device used to order the narrative.

2   Natural presentation: This organizational structure often is suited to presentation of findings from a synthesis that demonstrates a process. The findings are arranged in a way that mirrors the process, so that it is a natural sequencing of events or actions. The process may or may not be a linear one, but the key elements are identified and presented in sequence.

3   Central concept: If the synthesis uncovered a central or umbrella concept, the content of the narrative may be organized around it. In this approach, the central concept is generally treated initially and sub-concepts are introduced while demonstrating how they support the central concept.

4   Most important to least important: We find that in syntheses, some concepts are more prevalent than others, but often the presentation treats them as if they are of equal weight. Presenting them from most important to least important provides the reader with a sense of scale.

5   Most simple to most complex: This approach is useful for presenting complicated findings, particularly to busy readers who would appreciate a scaffolding effect. The findings are arranged from simple ideas building to more complex concepts, which require more unpacking.

6   Theory-guided: As we noted above, synthesists may wish to use a conceptual or theoretical frame to guide interpretations. If this is done, then the theory may provide a logical structure for sequencing themes and concepts.

These strategies are logical ways to structure findings, but they are only effective if exemplars demonstrate their efficacy as devices. Exemplars are often events, observations, actions, details or examples that illustrate synthesists' accuracy in interpreting the data. We believe that exemplars are best conveyed through use of thick description, which we describe in the next section.

Data as central: Thick description

The narrative that we describe above should be punctuated with data. This data should be included in the form of rich, thick description. Leading sociologist Clifford Geertz popularized the notion of thick description while describing his approach to ethnography (Geertz, 1973), although Ryle (1968), who believed that the concept of culture was critical in social science research and thus worthy of attention, was the originator of the term. Geertz's description of his concept involved explanation of the context as well as the importance of interpretation. Geertz's definition of thick description involved observation of social life captured through dense descriptions, which thereby allowed for generalization and interpretation. Ryle first used the term to attribute intentionality to behaviour. He used the following example, of an apparently male golfer:

> A single golfer, with six golf balls in front of him, hitting each of them, one after another, towards one and the same green. He then goes and collects the balls, comes back to where he was before and does it again. What is he doing?
>
> (Ryle, 1971: 474)

If not thick, this description would merely be 'The golfer keeps hitting the ball with a club'. The thick description reveals the interpretation of the behaviour within several interlaid contexts: the game of golf, the golf course, the person. The researcher's next step then is to assign intentionality to the golfer's behaviour, including considerations such as why such behaviour is occurring and what the subtext might be (Ponterotto, 2006).

Denzin developed the concept of thick description further and argued that it:

> does more than record what a person is doing. It goes beyond mere fact and surface appearances. It presents detail, context, emotion and the webs of social relationships that join persons to one another. Thick description evokes emotionality and self-feelings. It inserts history into experience. It establishes the significance of an experience, or the sequence of events, for the person or persons in question. In thick description, the voices, feelings, actions and meanings of interacting individuals are heard.
>
> (Denzin, 1989: 83)

Thick description is not just reporting detail, but instead demands interpretation that goes beyond meaning and motivations. It is critical then for both plausibility and for making the narrative compelling.

We should note that in presenting original data and thick description in syntheses, different original qualitative studies seldom are identified by citational information (Paterson et al., 2001); the results are synthesis after all, so the argument is that it is the combination that is of interest rather than keeping track of which study had which finding. However, some researchers have maintained the distinct identity of the different studies (Major, 2010). It is up to synthesists to determine which approach is more appropriate for the goal that they are trying to accomplish. We believe, however, that it is important to find some way to make the distinctions amongst studies, whether by indicating original study by name, number or some other signifier such as geographic location. Not only does this help maintain the participant voices but it also provides referents for the audience, much in the way that using pseudonyms in original studies would.

Visual displays

In addition to the narrative, visual representations can be effective in presenting findings, particularly complex findings, and in showing the connections and relationships between concepts. Several different graphic organizers can help make narrative information visually appealing and easily understood. We identify some of these in the following sections.

Tables and charts

Tables and charts represent the simplest type of graphic organizer. They allow for condensing and organizing data about many themes into rows or columns. Tables provide important structure and sequencing that makes the logic trail easier for readers to follow. Table 6.4 comes from Savin-Baden et al. (2008) in which overarching themes are identified.

The disadvantage of a chart like this is that it is difficult to discern how one theme was translated into another.

Processes and flow charts

If the topic or concept being studied or that emerged during study is a process, particularly one with a single beginning and multiple possible outcomes, then a flowchart can be a useful graphic organizer. The figure that we included at the end of Chapter 4, presented again here, is an example of a flowchart, showing an interlocking relationship between the processes (Figure 6.1).

The complexity of a diagram like this makes it difficult to see details.

Table 6.4 Indication of themes and levels of analysis

Overarching themes	Second order interpretations	Third order interpretations
Practice	Improving practice Changing practice The impact of innovation Creation of theory Understanding students Staff experiences	Identity Agency Disjunction Academic stances Notions of improvement Learning spaces Academic cultures Communities of practice
Community	Disciplinary communities Online/e-learning communities Education development communities Inquiry-based learning communities	
Transfer	Transfer for shared practice Transfer related to policy	

Hierarchies and figures

When it is important to show relationships between findings or when findings become unwieldy in a table format, figures can serve a useful purpose. Figures can transform tables into visual representations of the concepts. Such figures can also allow one to demonstrate the process of moving from first order analysis to

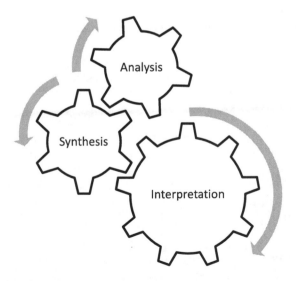

Figure 6.1 Example of flow chart.

second order interpretations to third order interpretations. Consider the following example from Major's work on distance education:

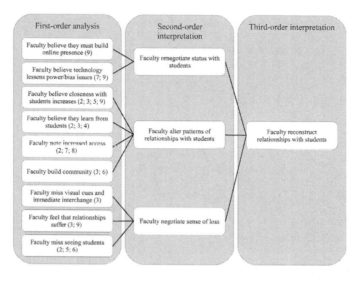

Figure 6.2 Illustration of hierarchies.

The challenge of this type of chart is that visually, all findings appear to be of equal weight. Major (2010) attempted to counter this challenge by indicating the studies that included the findings through use of a key, with study numbers indicated in parentheses.

Relationships and structures: Concept maps

Concept maps, as illustrated in Figure 6.3, are gaining in popularity among qualitative researchers. These can allow synthesists to show main themes, concepts and sub themes, as well as patterns of relationships.

The disadvantage is that these can be visually complicated and confusing.

Although difficulties exist with whatever visual display is chosen, all of these have an overriding benefit of presenting mass information in a quick, easy to read, visually appealing format. Any intended audience member will appreciate the clarity and brevity that they provide. Policy makers in particular may find them useful for quickly identifying concepts and ideas and potential connections between them.

The discussion

In developing a discussion section, synthesists go beyond the presentation of findings and are able to spend time providing a rationale for them, as they

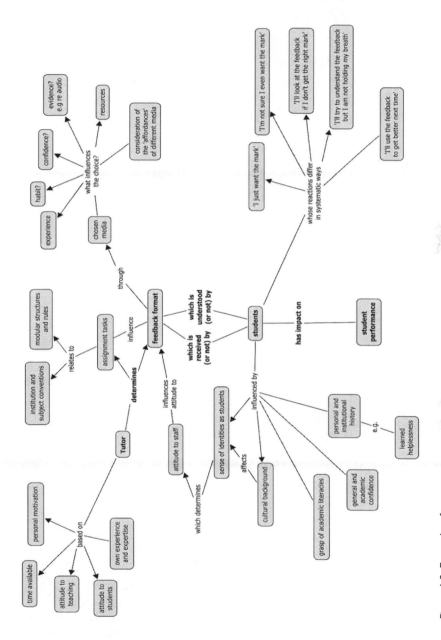

Figure 6.3 Example of a concept map.

articulate ways in which the interpretations are supported. We believe that this section should contain three key areas: a discussion of the findings, recommendations for research and recommendations for practice and policy. These areas are described more fully in the next few sections.

Connection of findings to theory and literature

A discussion section generally begins with highlights of the key themes. Synthesists illuminate the themes as well as their significance to the overall synthesis. Many times, synthesists connect themes to other literature. Synthesists may make connections to a theoretical body of knowledge. Connections also may be made to quantitative literature, showing how the synthesis extends those findings. Finally, connections may be made with other qualitative literature, showing how the findings support, refute or build a bridge to connect related concepts. The general discussion then can tie together large bodies of knowledge for the reader, making important connections that the findings have demonstrated.

Recommendations for research

In making recommendations for further research, synthesists have an opportunity to drive the development of a field of study or discipline, by saying where the research has led and what it has shown. Furthermore, synthesists often have a sense of the location of problematic areas in the literature and can indicate how the research should be improved. Several key areas for synthesists to consider include whether there are

- different people/stakeholders who should be interviewed;
- different environments that should be examined;
- similar conditions/events/processes/subjects that should be studied;
- methodological gaps that are apparent.

Such considerations can drive the development of future research and thus knowledge production. This review, however, must be done with grace and caution. It is equally important for synthesists to indicate what has been done well in the research as it is to point out what should be done.

Recommendations for policy and practice

The findings generally are intended not only to prompt conversations and debates in the literature, but also to inform policy and practice. The section on recommendations for policy and practice is often the section most read by policy makers and busy academics. They often are the most difficult to write, however, not only because they induce a shift in the way researchers think about findings but also because of the confusion over what policies actually are and lack of information about how to make recommendations for them. We recommend thinking about the differences between policies, procedures and guidelines, which we define below.

- Policies are strategies, rules and principles intended to guide actions.
- Procedures involve an action or set of actions that are necessary to implement policies.
- Guidelines are statements of procedures required to carry out policies, usually written in abridged form and made widely available.

Synthesists can focus on any or all of these for making recommendations for policy.

To illustrate our point, we offer the following example. In Major's article (2010) about staff experiences online, her intended audience was university administrators. She found that staff who participate in distance learning change their views of their roles. Thus, she made several recommendations, which may be thought of as influencing policy, procedure and guidelines as shown in Table 6.5.

Table 6.5 Recommendations for influencing policy, procedure and guidelines

Policy	Staff who are planning to teach online should be prepared for a change in roles
Procedure	Staff who are planning to use distance learning will participate in staff development workshops describing how roles may change online
Guideline	The university requires that staff who teach online will participate in a staff development orientation workshop, as outlined in the online staff handbook

In recommendations for future policy and practice, then, synthesists have the opportunity to discuss how their findings can contribute to important changes in these areas, as well as to outline specific steps or actions that should be taken.

The conclusion

The conclusion is an opportunity for a final word with the reader and thus is a space to argue for the importance of the study. There are several strategies that synthesists can employ when developing a conclusion. We offer a few suggestions for consideration:

- Conclude by returning to the ideas, concepts, examples, facts or themes that have been presented in the introduction. While it is important to steer away from introducing new concepts, it also is important to provide a sense of completeness of the study, and returning to initial concepts can help the reader feel that the synthesis has been tied together and provide a sense of closure.
- Summarize the key points or findings from the paper. While it is important that synthesists do not rely on the conclusion to summarize the important

points by repeating them verbatim, a brief summary can help reiterate and reinforce the 'take away' points.

- Acknowledge the lack of conclusion. Often synthesists feel like they have assumed a position of knowing 'the answers'. After all, the point of synthesis is to gain a comprehensive picture by drawing together findings from multiple studies. However, it is just as important to acknowledge when there is no definite conclusion to be made. Indeed often what is found during a synthesis is that there are more questions to be asked and this is a valid concluding point as well.
- Ensure that the 'so what' question has been answered. The synthesis should take care to make sure that the study has some implications. This can be accomplished, for example, by ensuring the importance of the study and its implications are presented clearly.
- Speculate on the future of the topic and make inferences for the direction it will go. Synthesists have assumed the role of authority (in a manner of speaking) on a given topic and thus have the important task of discussing where the future of the work lies.
- Consider the methodological implications of the work. While the subject matter is important, the process of qualitative research synthesis is still being developed. Thus we believe it is important for synthesists to spend time discussing the methodological issues that arose during the work, not in small part to provide future synthesists with sound advice.

While these are among a range of suggestions, ultimately, what is included in a conclusion is dependent upon synthesis goals, the intended audience, the findings and their implications and the methodological issues that arose during the study. At its heart, though, the conclusion should function to provide a sense of closure and leave the reader with a lasting impression of the study.

Conclusion

In this chapter, we have suggested some ways in which a synthesis may be presented. We have used as our orienting concept the idea that synthesists should focus the attention on the intended audience and make decisions about their presentation that best represent the study's goals and findings while speaking directly to this audience. The underlying idea is that it is critical to gain audience attention and interest in order to achieve the greatest impact with the synthesis.

Conclusion

In this conclusion to Parts 1 and 2, we consider our rationale for this book. The next few sections, then, reprise our reasons for writing this book. In the final section of this conclusion we describe Part 3 of this book, along with presenting our rationale for including it.

The call to synthesize

With the arrival of the 21st century, scholars have seen a host of forces at work, many of which hold the potential to influence the course of social science research. Among these forces are the desire to advance knowledge, the increased need for knowledge about the success or failure of interventions in professional practical arenas, the increased demand for accountability in practice professions, and the decreased resources available to fund research. Due to these forces, along with others who have taken up this call, we believe it vital that we begin to make the best use of research findings. By best use, we mean that research findings generally should not only drive theory but also add to an actionable knowledge base. Thus we believe that efforts toward synthesis specifically should serve to educate researchers, practitioners and policy makers alike. We, like others, believe that synthesis has this potential to accomplish these goals because of the value it can add to current research practices. Suri and Clarke (2009) explain this potential value like this:

> The value-addedness of a research synthesis lies to a significant extent in its ability to bring to light new ways of looking at a set of primary research studies. The evidence of a research synthesis is more complex, refined, and sophisticated. A research synthesis advances knowledge in a field by identifying transcendental features and patterns across a number of studies ... Subtle nuances that form the essence of a phenomenon can become noticeable through systematic comparisons, to make explicit similarities and variations between individual studies examining that phenomenon. Research synthesis plays an important role in informing policy, practice, public perception, and further research by making explicit connections between individual studies ...

> In sum, research synthesis is a methodology in its own right, involving numer-
> ous tasks and critical decisions. Efforts and resources required in a rigorous
> research synthesis are comparable to those required in a rigorous primary
> study
>
> (Suri and Clarke, 2009: 406)

We agree with the benefits of synthesis that Suri and Clarke and other scholars
espouse as well as their assessments of the complexity involved in conducting a
synthesis.

While quantitative researchers have adopted a range of approaches synthesizing existing research findings, including meta-analysis and systematic review,
qualitative researchers have been somewhat slower to take up the change. The
reasons for this are many. Some researchers, for example, have adopted the justi-
fiable perspective, one to which we are sympathetic, that no single 'truth' exists
and thus synthesis efforts that seek to discover greater meaning across studies
hold little value to them. Some researchers see it as their duty to seek to provide
competing accounts and evidence, and qualitative research synthesis which can in
some ways reconcile or explain competing accounts is contrary to their purposes.
Some have never seen the approach applied in practice and thus have never considered it an option. And some have found it a complex process for which few
guides and examples exist.

On the other hand, the convergence of these forces has caused a fundamental shift in the way that a growing number of qualitative scholars think about
research. Many have begun to understand their charge differently. Rather than
an exercise of conducting research for research's sake, they have begun to view
research as a purposeful enterprise that can help address current professional
practice and policy needs. They have identified it is as an important goal to find
ways of using qualitative studies effectively, by taking a wider view of issues, by
using global studies rather than tending to focus only on local ones, and by viewing findings collectively, as quantitative researchers have been able to do. These
scholars have adopted a range of approaches to synthesizing qualitative research,
which we described more fully in Chapter 2. To date, however, many qualitative researchers who have made a mental shift toward valuing goals that may be
achieved through qualitative research synthesis have found it difficult to compile
findings from small scale studies to best advantage.

We believe that those who adopt qualitative research synthesis (will) find
several distinct advantages to the approach, many of which we have outlined in
Chapter 1 and throughout this book, that provide both immediate benefits to
the individual researchers as well as long range benefits that can appeal to the
greater good. By using qualitative research synthesis as an approach, further,
synthesists can gain both a wide and detailed view of a particular issue under
study. Adopting qualitative research synthesis also can allow qualitative studies to
be used to inform policy-making in ways that currently do not take place. When
using qualitative research synthesis in the future, it will be possible to draw on

data sets of similar types and offer findings that are not only more transferrable but also that deal with reasonably large data sets and more diverse populations. While we recognize that qualitative research at first can seem hard work and time consuming because of the complexity, we believe it is an important approach which will help ensure that qualitative studies, particularly interpretive ones, are valued, used and funded in the future.

Essential features of qualitative research synthesis

We recommend in this conclusion that there are several features that are essential to qualitative research. We developed these from our own work while also considering the suggestions of Suri and Clarke (2009), who advocate for a set of methodologically inclusive criteria for syntheses which they developed through an analysis of the outstanding features of award winning efforts at synthesis. We offer the following criteria, which specifically relate to qualitative research synthesis, for consideration. While we necessarily have discussed these issues in more depth throughout the book, we reprise them here in a final overview as we further extend some of the ideas.

The topic undertaken should be substantive

As we have advocated throughout this text as well as in this conclusion, qualitative research should investigate topics that are of practical value to stakeholder groups. This means that the topic should not only be timely and meaningful, as may be evident in professional practice literature, but also that it has been subject to on-going investigation, which should be clear enough during the review of the literature phase. As we describe in Chapter 3, the question should be one that yields a sufficient number of robust studies. It is important then for the synthesist to consider whether, and to document that, the existing research base was substantive enough for the goal of synthesis to be accomplished.

Previous literature on the topic should be reviewed critically

Synthesists should ensure that existing literature, including other syntheses as well as primary studies related to the topic, were investigated with a critical eye. This means that they not only located the literature and read it carefully, but also that they evaluated the body of work. Assuming the role of critic, then, we mean that the synthesist should have approached the literature from an analytical perspective, and judged it for its plausibility and for its contribution to the knowledge base. Existing research and literature reviews, further, should have been acknowledged and explained in the final presentation of the synthesis, as we describe in Chapter 6.

The search process should be well planned, executed, and documented. One of the values of syntheses generally and of qualitative research synthesis specifically, is its reliance upon a rigorous and methodologically-grounded approach. As we suggested in Chapter 3, we assert that research bias is inherent in design and that it should be acknowledged and kept to the fore during the design process. All processes further should be documented and resulting products should ensure that these processes were shared with the intended audience. We believe it essential for synthesists to acknowledge their stances throughout the process and in the final documentation.

The approach to analysis should be an interpretive one

One characteristic of all syntheses, as we describe in Chapter 2, is that they break down information and reassemble it into some sort of whole. Quantitative approaches tend to view parts that relate to the whole, while qualitative tend to view aggregates of the individual parts. Qualitative research synthesis further requires interpretation. For us, interpretation means acknowledging that synthesists have approached the work subjectively and that they simply have sought to discover the meaning the authors and participants themselves have assigned to various findings, by considering research in aggregate.

We acknowledge the debate in the literature that considers the question of whether synthesis should be aggregative or interpretive. And we understand the differing perspectives and points of view. However, along with Gough and Elbourne (2002) we believe that this debate has the potential to be unnecessarily polarizing. We all are engaged in the common goal of making meaning of qualitative studies collectively, after all, and thus we have the potential to learn from each other. Further we recognize that different questions require different processes. However, we believe that all efforts to synthesize qualitative studies by nature require some interpretation. Thus we believe that even the most contentious efforts toward objectivity and aggregation in qualitative synthesis actually have required some interpretation (while acknowledging that others do not hold this belief). We see it then as a scale of interpretivisim, with synthesists on one end seeking to be as objective as possible then moving toward synthesists on the other end who not only allow for but also demand acknowledging an interpretive stance when engaging with data. We have already articulated and now reassert our placement on the scale as tending toward the latter end.

The resulting synthesis should be conceptually or theoretically grounded

The approaches to grounding a qualitative research synthesis are many and range from using grounded theory to letting themes emerge to grounding interpretations in an existing and well-established theory. The former has the benefit of truly seeking the meaning in the data alone. The latter has the benefit of using existing theory as a lens through which to view data and understand them. We advocate for a middle ground in Chapter 4 as we describe how to analyse data to let themes emerge and in Chapter 6 in which we describe the usefulness of drawing upon a theoretical frame. We argue that whatever the approach taken, the synthesist should have made a strong argument for it and should have acknowledged the argument and decision in the presentation of the synthesis.

Implications should be made explicit

We have argued throughout this book that syntheses should not only have implications for research but also for policy and practice. In Chapter 6, we asserted that identifying the intended audience can not only guide important decisions during the synthesis process but that it also can help guide recommendations not only for future research but also for policy and practice. Here we reassert that these implications are critical. Further, we assert that such data can allow for policies to be developed that have been drawn from studies that seek to research *with* people, and seek to understand people's lives – rather than only drawing upon research that begins with a hypothesis that is based upon the researcher's conjecture. Such a turn should mean that future policy meets the needs of people more effectively, because it is user-generated and user-focussed. Governments across the globe are increasingly interested in user-guided research, which is necessarily qualitative in its stance and process. However, without using qualitative research synthesis we risk missing opportunities to provide policy and practice solutions that really do make a difference to a range of stakeholder groups. Thus these implications should have been made explicit in recounting the findings in the final presentation.

The importance of disseminating methods and findings

Qualitative research synthesis represents a small but growing tradition within methods that undertake the task of synthesizing existing findings from qualitative studies. While in Chapter 2 we outlined a number of social science fields in which the methodology is seeing increasing use, we believe that it has potential for use in any of the social science disciplines. Further, we believe that such an approach has several potential final forms, each of which has the potential to improve dissemination of findings as well as methodology.

1   *Articles in peer reviewed journals.* While it can be true at times that top tier peer reviewed journals are read by few, the fact is that the ones who are reading them tend to be leading researchers in the field; they are the ones who contribute to these journals as well. Thus to have an impact on a field, and to take hold as a methodology, it is important to seek dissemination of syntheses in these journals. Through the resources we will share in Part 3 of this book, we demonstrate that syntheses can be published in leading journals in a variety of fields.

2   *Summaries for professional practice journals.* Practitioner journals tend to be the ones that more people, practitioners and even researchers, read, cite and share. Because of this, they can have a tremendous impact on professional practice. Summaries of qualitative research synthesis can be particularly effective in these potential dissemination outlets.

3   *Policy briefs for policy makers.* Policy briefs tend to be requested by those who need information that can allow them to choose, from a number of alternatives, a particular course of action. These briefs can be written from a more neutral perspective or can set up an argument of the choice of a particular course of action. In the past, policy briefs have not been able to use information from qualitative studies well, but this is improving with the development of approaches to synthesizing qualitative information. The benefit is putting findings directly in the hands of those who will make decisions based upon them.

4   *Master theses or PhD dissertations.* Meta-analysis has long been viewed as appropriate as a methodological approach for a dissertation or thesis. Here again efforts at qualitative synthesis are gaining ground. We made the decision to only include published works in our bibliography in Part 3 but acknowledge that an increasing number of candidates are using qualitative research synthesis as an approach. Frequently stakeholders turn to dissertations because they contain more extensive literature reviews than articles in peer reviewed or practitioner journals. Candidates taking up this methodology also have the advantage of learning how to use the approach, one which they can draw upon again during their careers, as either scholars or scholar-practitioners.

5   *Final paper at the BSc, MSc, or doctoral level.* We argued in our Introduction and intimated in Chapter 2 that qualitative research synthesis can be an appropriate assignment in lieu of a traditional research paper or research review. We have evidence of its effectiveness in this form because Claire has used qualitative research synthesis as a course assignment in her Doctoral-level seminars. She notes that it provides students with hands on experience with a research paper that requires data analysis and higher order thinking without the need to collect more primary data, which students do not have time for in the timeframe of a traditional semester. She finds that these papers often not only provide students with hands on experience with research processes but also that they frequently provide a springboard for longer papers to be done for a thesis or dissertation, as we described above. Further, some of the students have sought publications of their papers, allowing for dissemination of the findings as well as for positioning students as scholars.

Thus, presenting syntheses in peer reviewed scholarly articles as well as through alternative forms can enhance the circulation and thus use of findings.

Identifying cautions and caveats for using qualitative research synthesis

We argue that qualitative research synthesis is a rigorous methodology that has been refined over two decades of efforts. It has a set of procedures that ensure that the methodology has been achieved. Yet it is also flexible and adaptable, depending upon synthesists' needs and the demands of the research question. Qualitative research synthesis, as we have argued throughout this text, has the potential to be an important tool in the scholar's toolkit.

The question for qualitative researchers in social science fields to consider is whether we are sufficiently advanced methodologically to undertake such an approach. We have argued here for the approach and further argue that not only are we are ready for it, but also that it is necessary at this point in our development to help us make sense of the existing bodies of research and to point out future directions for our work, as well as to help refine the qualitative processes involved in both primary research (as gaps and omissions are identified) and in qualitative synthesis, as the approach becomes more refined over time.

In addition to the challenges that we identified in Chapter 1, we note here that because the quality of a qualitative research synthesis necessarily depends upon the quality of the primary studies, there is an inherent challenge in its design. Namely, if the primary studies are not sound, neither will be the synthesis. Moreover, the quality of the synthesis is dependent upon the transparency and reporting of the process and upon applying sound qualitative criteria for research and ensuring plausibility, which we outline in Chapter 6, yet the methodology is still evolving. Thus, we argue that when applied appropriately and carefully to a sound body of research, qualitative research synthesis can provide valuable insights; otherwise, it has the potential to do more harm than good.

Encouraging discussion about qualitative research synthesis

As we asserted in our introduction, we hope that this book encourages conversation and debate about qualitative research synthesis. We believe that such scholarly conversations are essential for qualitative research synthesis to be developed and refined.

Final reflection

This book is intended to be a user-friendly guide. Part 1 offered an overview of the approach as we envision it and situated it in the growing arena of synthesis of qualitative work. Part 2 provided step by step guidance on carrying out the approach, with details and examples, many times from our own work.

In Part 3 of this text, to which we turn next, we present examples of qualitative syntheses. These examples comprise executive summaries of our own syntheses, from which we have included examples throughout this book. We also include our first full length qualitative synthesis in its entirety. We further provide annotations to this article that contain critical comments about the ways in which we approached it. The reader thus can see how we applied our approach initially and how our views of it have evolved over time. Finally, we include a bibliography of texts about and published examples of qualitative syntheses of qualitative research. Rather than providing examples of only those that claim to be interpretive or meta-ethnographic, in an effort toward inclusivity, we also provide citations for those works that claim to be more aggregative in approach. These studies informed our thinking about our approach, so we believe they may have use to others. Further, we believe that including them allows us to provide the reader with the greatest exposure to those who have approached qualitative synthesis of qualitative research in a range of fields and that we can learn by the efforts of all of us who have attempted this task.

Part 3

Resources

Examples of studies using qualitative research synthesis

Savin-Baden, M.; Macfarlane, L. and Savin-Baden, J. (2008) Learning spaces, agency and notions of improvement: Influencing thinking and practices about teaching and learning in higher education. An interpretive meta-ethnography, *London Review of Education*, 6(3): 211–229.

This review was intended to identify key themes related to influencing thinking and practices about teaching and learning in higher education, indicate how these understandings can inform the higher education community and make recommendations to guide policy, practice and research. In particular, it set out to explore the following questions:

- What does the literature indicate about teaching and learning thinking and practices in higher education?
- What are the tensions and differences across practices and communities, for example e-learning communities or problem-based learning communities?
- What is the relationship between theories of teaching and learning and actual practices?

The review mapped the literature, including evaluative reports produced by development agencies and practitioners, to clarify the ways in which knowledge transfer can and does take place and the conditions under which it is most likely to occur. The review also examined the nature and extent of engagement with these ideas in the literature intended for three 'stakeholder' groups: academic teaching staff (practitioners), institutional policy makers and educational developers.

Background literature

This review examined three broad areas of literature to set the context for the meta-ethnography:

- Critical awareness tradition, espoused by theorists such as Freire (1972, 1974), hooks (1994) and Pratt (1998).

- Cognitivism and critical awareness, espoused by theorists such as Barnett (1987, 1990, 1994, 2000a, 2000b).
- Discipline-based pedagogy, as described by Jenkins and Zetter (2003) and Meyer and Land (2003, 2004).

Methodology

The literature was initially categorized into the following three core themes:

- Practice: the idea of practice was examined and the review considered the literature that explores the nature of teaching and learning practices, including those that are tacit and those that are highly situated. Issues in the identification of 'good' and 'best practice' were highlighted; conceptions that are open to critique.
- Transfer: literature that critiques ideas about transfer, and thus offers a sophisticated understanding of issues in knowledge transfer, was examined. Further, the study also examined the possibilities for and realities of transfer, across both knowledge domains and areas of practice. A mapping of conceptions of and approaches to change, particularly in academic contexts, gave this part of the review a wider base in the literature on change.
- Community: literature that relates to an understanding of the communities was reviewed, including literature on the following concepts: academic identity, networks and communities of practice, knowledge management and the role and orientations of change agents, including educational development agencies and practitioners.

This review used interpretive meta-ethnography as its methodology. This is a qualitative approach to managing a large range of literature, from the interpretivist tradition. It presents an analysis of the findings across studies and then interprets it in relation to further themes that emerge across studies.

Interpretive meta-ethnography is thus a systematic approach that enables comparison, analysis and interpretations to be made that can inform theorizing and practice. Noblit and Hare (1988) suggested, by acknowledging researchers as interpretivists, that it is possible to recover the social and theoretical context of research and thus reveal further noteworthy findings. Interpretive meta-ethnography involves developing inclusion and exclusion criteria, applying these to studies and then applying a three-stage process (Savin-Baden and Major, 2007), for managing, analysing and interpreting the selected studies.

Identification, selection and analysis of the literature

This literature review used the innovative approach of meta-ethnography of each theme at three levels: level 1 searching and analysing articles to include and exclude; level 2 locating articles in relation to core themes and subthemes through different levels of analysis; and level 3 synthesising data. At level 1, the initial search yielded over 6,000 articles, edited collections and monographs, which were culled to 83 studies by a process of applying predetermined inclusion and exclusion criteria. At level 2, annotations, maps, tables and grids were used to identify and connect studies with the key themes. At level 3, data were analysed by interpretative comparison and inductive analysis. References to the three primary themes were mapped for each area of literature. Data were then analysed to gain second-order interpretations and to develop third-order interpretations that synthesised the issues across the studies; the themes of practice, transfer and community; and the three areas of practitioner, policy and development communities.

Findings of overall synthesis from the literature

These issues identified in the review shed light on areas that would bear further research and exploration, and that in many cases need to be focused on more frequently by those involved in thinking about teaching and learning. The primary third order themes that emerged from analysis and interpretation were as follows:

- Pedagogical stance (i.e. the choices and interventions that faculty make within a learning environment derived from their concerns).
- Disjunction (i.e. a sense of being stuck within a given teaching paradigm).
- Learning spaces (i.e. the notion that there are unique spaces within the academic environment in which learning occurs).
- Agency (i.e. the way a person's expectations and aspirations influence their choices in how they execute their roles).
- Notions of improvement (i.e. an individual's impressions of how improvement should be undertaken. This could involve improvements imposed by an institution, improvement because of a governmental agenda, bottom-up and top-down improvement).
- Communities of interest (i.e. the social learning that occurs amongst groups with shared interests).

Recommendations

From the review, the authors made the following recommendations for practice and policy:

1   There is a need to develop commonly-understood discourses about teaching and learning, as a prerequisite to being able to make teaching and learning regimes explicit and challenging them openly.
2   There remains relatively little understanding of the impact of disciplinary differences across teaching and learning research and practices and this requires further research.

3   The professionalisation of teaching remains problematic and requires further research and changes in funding and university practices to engage with this.
4   E-learning pedagogy is largely missing from the literature and needs to be developed and researched.
5   Research into learning spaces requires further study.

Conclusion

This review helped to identify overarching themes and subthemes that influence practice, transfer and community. The literature that it examined is often underused in the processes of design and decision making. However, the authors note the tendency to privilege similarity with this type of approach and thus urge readers to view their interpretation as contestable.

Major, C. (2010). Do virtual professors dream of electric students? College faculty experiences with online distance education, *Teachers College Record*, 112(8).

Over time, faculty have held a key role in determining distance learning's success or failure in institutions of higher education. Faculty acceptance of current online technologies has yet to be demonstrated. Indeed, leading scholars suggest that a number of obstacles exist for faculty teaching online, including lack of established pedagogical practices, unease about careers and workloads, and added roles and responsibilities. For this reason, faculty experiences teaching online represent a potentially rich vein of information about the efficacy of online learning in higher education.

Quantitative research that has examined the phenomenon has tended to focus on faculty perceptions of advantages and disadvantages of online learning. Surveys show that faculty agree that potential professional advantages include flexibility and efficiency, opportunities to use new technologies, and intellectual challenges. They also agree that there are potential pedagogical advantages, such as increased opportunities to assume a facilitator role, improved knowledge of students, wider varieties of course offerings, and enhanced learning. Faculty also agreed that a number of potential professional disadvantages to online learning exist, including increased demands on time, inadequate compensation, lack of recognition and reward, and questions about intellectual property ownership. Faculty also note organizational challenges, including lack of appropriate hardware, software, and technical support. They also agree that there are potential pedagogical disadvantages, including perceptions of lower course quality, decreased interaction with students, lack of visual clues to help read students, lack of student familiarity with technology, and increased academic dishonesty.

While these findings are important, these quantitative studies do not present rich, thick description of the lived experiences of faculty teaching in online environments. Investigating how faculty experience online teaching is critical to understanding new practices and patterns of behavior that occur in the technology-mediated environment. Qualitative studies that systematically examine the experiences of faculty who have taught online, then, represent a potential source of information about online distance education.

Methodology

The purpose of this research was to employ a rigorous and systematic approach to make meaning of individual qualitative studies by considering them in aggregate and thus to glean the important lessons that they have to offer collectively. Using a meta-synthesis approach meant following several specific steps. The first step involved identifying and selecting studies through online databases and hand-searching tables of contents of key instructional technology journals. The second step involved selecting studies for inclusion based upon a set of predetermined criteria; 9 studies that comprise 23 authors from 5 countries and 117 faculty were included. The third step involved using meta-ethnographic techniques for data analysis and synthesis; it relied upon analysis techniques common to meta-ethnographic approaches, including reciprocal translation analysis (translating themes into each other), refutations synthesis (attempting to explain variations and contradictions), and lines-of-argument analysis (building a general interpretation from findings of separate studies through reliance on qualitative analysis such as constant comparison). The fourth step involved using a conceptual frame, Zuboff *In the Age of the Smart Machine* (1984), as a lens for data interpretation; Zuboff asserts that computer-based technologies are not neutral but rather impose as well as produce new patterns of information and social relations.

Findings

Faculty change public presentation of selves

Faculty in several of the studies indicated that when teaching online they were confronted by challenging situations that caused them to reconsider who they were as teachers and how they presented themselves in the technology-mediated environment. Such confrontation often led to changes in teaching stance, teaching role, and teaching personas. Faculty in several studies noted that their beliefs about teacher centrality to the learning process shifted. Changes in roles and perspectives led them to develop new teaching skills. Faculty noted additional feelings of accountability online, in part due to the permanence of the written word (even though online), and they often became more careful in crafting responses.

Faculty feel professional rejuvenation from teaching online

Faculty articulated a sense of professional renewal when teaching online. Many faculty noted, however, that initially they felt like they were stepping into the unknown. They lacked knowledge about their undertakings, so they did not always appreciate the difficulty of teaching online or the technology's potential and power. Most faculty tended to overcome initial trepidation and engage with technology in extended ways. Many of the faculty described a renewed appreciation of the complexity of teaching that came with teaching courses online. They described a sense of intellectual challenge that attended developing new ideas and skill sets. The technology afforded faculty with the opportunity to learn. Faculty often discussed the creative aspect of teaching online.

Faculty increase structure in online courses

Faculty believed that teaching online led to an increased need to structure. They talked about having to think through a course from start to finish. They talked of scaffolding information for students. They also described an increased need to anticipate student actions and responses and to prepare for them. The reasons for increasing structure were many and included increasing efficiency and improving learning. Faculty noted mixed success on achieving these goals. Faculty further noted that the additional structure often caused feelings of loss of spontaneity.

Faculty assume additional responsibilities when teaching online

Faculty in several of the studies believed that they assumed additional responsibilities when teaching online. Among these responsibilities were managing students' technology and managing expectations for online participation. They also described increased requirements for learning and using technology and new duties involving working with technology staff.

Faculty feel increased demands on time

Faculty described the myriad ways in which demands on their time increased. They noted that work seemed constant and often impeded on personal time. They noted increases in the amount of time they spent, both developing courses and teaching online. Corresponding with students through emails and postings created the greatest increased demand on time, and providing individual feedback on each written assignment came in second. Faculty believed that increased time took a toll on other professional activities, particularly research.

Faculty reconstruct relationships with students

Faculty described a number of ways in which their relationships with students changed. They often found that they had to renegotiate their professional status with students. They noted benefits in being freed from preconceptions that students might hold about them and that they might hold about their students. They also described a sense of being closer to their students, particularly at an intellectual level. Many faculty noted increased appreciation for students, suggesting that they could draw upon student experiences when teaching and could view students as partners in the learning process. Many faculty, however, articulated an inability to draw upon relationship-building tools that had served them in the past. A number of faculty simply missed seeing students.

Discussion

Finding new ways to understand existing literature was one of the primary goals of this study. These results represent a starting place for improving current practice as well as for guiding future research, particularly for those working in similar contexts to the faculty interviewed in the articles included in the study. Future research should strive to add depth to the field by focusing on single and specific issues related to the teaching experience, recognizing different types of online learning (i.e. asynchronous, synchronous, or blended), and investigating differences between various types of institutions. Future research in this area also should strive to make questions of transferability and credibility more answerable by more clearly articulating research designs, using established techniques for data presentation, and making issues of researcher positionality clear. Practitioners should seek to collaborate with faculty to ease changes in roles, focus on the creative aspects of teaching online, provide time-management support, and prepare faculty for shifting relationships with students.

Conclusion

The title of this article, "Do virtual professors dream of electric students? College faculty experiences with online distance education," not only alludes to the title of Philip K. Dick's science fiction novel *Do Androids Dream of Electric Sheep?* but in so doing also raises the question of what it means to teach online. The findings suggest that faculty appeared to create new personas online, with an individual ultimately evolving as a "virtual professor." The term "electric" could describe how faculty viewed online students, views which ranged from enthusiastic about the energy they exhibit to troubled by feelings of remoteness. The term "dream" underscores a central question of this work: whether faculty really *want* to teach online, whether they dream of being virtual professors interacting with electric students. This research suggests that no easy answer exists but rather it depends upon whether faculty effectively use technology for establishing connections and reconstituting social relations. The findings of this study represent a starting place for improving current practice, for guiding future research, and for continued conversations about the methodology of qualitative synthesis.

Executive summaries of qualitative meta-synthesis articles

SAMPLE PAPER
(Reprinted with permission)

Savin-Baden, M., and Major, C. H. (2007). Using interpretive meta-ethnography to explore the relationship between innovative approaches to learning and innovative methods of pedagogical research. *Higher Education*, 54(6): 833–852.

Text	Author comments
Using interpretative meta-ethnography to explore the relationship between innovative approaches to learning and their influence on faculty understanding of teaching	We selected a title that indicates the broader topic as well as the methodological approach. While we did not view it as a methods paper per se and thus did not want to give primacy to the methods over the content, we felt it important to identify the approach, not only because of its significance, but also so that it would be easily identifiable to others searching for papers using similar approaches.
Introduction	
Recent developments in approaches to teaching and learning, such as problem-based learning (PBL), project-based learning, and action learning, have led to new inquiry into how these methods affect the faculty who employ them. This trend, coupled with new developments in interpretive and qualitative methods, provides a rich vein of possible lenses to add to our understanding, and we are beginning to see research in this direction. Yet few researchers have integrated findings across qualitative studies that have explored faculty experiences of PBL, an area ripe for such investigation. This paper undertakes such a project but shifts away from quantitative forms of meta-analysis and quasi-qualitative forms of meta-synthesis and instead adopts interpretative meta-ethnography as the research framework.	We introduced the topic, intimating the primary intended audience of researchers and acknowledged the methodology for the approach.
Relevant literature	
Several streams of literature provide the context for this article: teacher knowledge, pedagogical content knowledge, discipline-based pedagogy, and faculty experience of PBL. These areas shed light on our understanding of how faculty may *know* about teaching and learning. They	We chose to include information in the relevant literature section that could serve as conceptual grounding for the

also provide us a framework for thinking about how faculty knowledge may change with time and experience.

study. These guiding concepts also helped to ground our interpretations.

This initial section was designed to provide strong context setting, partly because information about teacher knowledge was critical for readers to have in order to understand the findings. It was also to illustrate the breadth and depth of the literature available and to indicate to the readers that we were familiar with the areas under review.

While relatively new to higher education, research on teacher knowledge has been common in secondary education for some time. Teacher knowledge and beliefs about what to do, how to do it, and under which circumstances can affect the way that students learn a particular subject matter. Shulman's work (1986, 1987) provides a framework for understanding teacher knowledge in which he describes several layers that include both subject knowledge and pedagogical knowledge. Subject or content knowledge comprises the theories, principles, and concepts of a particular discipline. In addition to this subject matter knowledge, general pedagogical knowledge or knowledge about teaching itself is an important aspect of teacher knowledge. This general pedagogical knowledge has been the focus of most of the research on teaching. While subject knowledge and pedagogical knowledge are perhaps self-evident, Shulman (1986, p. 6) asks: 'why this sharp distinction between content and pedagogical process?' Somewhere between subject matter knowledge and pedagogical knowledge lies pedagogical content knowledge. Pedagogical content knowledge, he asserts, draws upon knowledge that is specific to teaching a particular subject matter and he describes pedagogical content knowledge as:

the ways of representing and formulating the subject that make it comprehensible to others ... Pedagogical content knowledge also includes an understanding of what makes the learning of specific topics easy or difficult: the conceptions and preconceptions that students of different ages and backgrounds bring with them to the learning of those most frequently taught topics and lessons. (Shulman 1986, pp. 9–10)

In the UK there has been increasing discussion about discipline-based pedagogy (which we suggest is parallel to pedagogical content knowledge) particularly in the debates about the relationship between research and teaching. Jenkins and Zetter (2003) argue that disciplines shape the nature of pedagogy and such pedagogies reflect the practices and culture of the discipline. Yet although we consider that discipline-based pedagogy requires more understanding and further unpacking, we believe as Delanty suggests, 'Disciplinary boundaries are becoming blurred as multidisciplinarity becomes the norm and as the new phenomenon of 'postdisciplinarity' takes over (Turner 1999)' (Delanty 2001, p. 3). Knowledge production is no longer situated just in academe but instead it takes place in hospitals, schools, communities and companies, as well as universities. However, what is not clear in the studies and discussions about discipline-based pedagogy is how it is that faculty break down disciplinary restrictions and instead search for more inter-disciplinary approaches. We suggest that research needs to be undertaken that examines the integrative character of discipline-based pedagogy. In particular, we should learn from those faculty who have all selected a particular educational approach because they believe it best supports teaching within an interdisciplinary context.	While teacher knowledge research developed in the US, a complimentary body of research developed in the UK, and since the articles in our study were set in both the US and the UK, we believed it critical to acknowledge this work as context. Further we were also aware that there is tendency to privilege work in one's country of origin and we wanted to stand against this.
One of the areas where we see the breaking down of disciplinary boundaries for both faculty and students is in PBL. Much of the research conducted in the area of problem-based learning has attempted focused on student outcomes, but recently studies have begun to focus on faculty experiences with the approach as well. Research indicates that using PBL has an influence on faculty members' perceptions of their teaching. For example, faculty who are familiar with problem-based learning favour it over other instructional methods (Albanese & Mitchell 1993; Vernon & Blake 1993).	The main catalyst for change of teacher knowledge in our studies was attempting problem-based learning; for this reason, we believed it critical to explore the approach briefly, particularly the research relating to teacher experiences with the methods. However, we were also aware there were relatively few in-depth interpretive studies in this area.

In a study of PBL faculty roles, Dahlgren, Castensson, and Dahlgren (1998) found that tutors' perceptions of their roles influenced their levels of satisfaction with PBL. What instructors know, or think they know, about the discipline, the course, and the students as learners affects their pedagogical choices (Major & Palmer 2006; Martin Prosser, Trigwell, Ramsden, & Benjamin 2000). However, the research stops short. It leaves us wondering what kind of changes to faculty thinking are required when moving to a PBL approach, and it is this question that we begin to explore here.

Methodology

Research design

Meta-analysis remains rare among those using collaborative and interpretative inquiry, and few researchers have undertaken an integration of findings from these kinds of studies. Those who have undertaken such a task have tended either to impose the frameworks and values of quantitative systematic reviews on qualitative studies or have moved toward the use of meta-synthesis. The use of systematic reviews, of whatever sort, implies that the drawing up of a set of rules for 'systematically' reviewing evidence will necessarily make the process of the review and research transparent. Yet there are degrees of transparency and points beyond which it is not possible to go when undertaking such reviews. The difficulty with meta-analysis that is not located in an interpretive tradition is the propensity to decontextualize material, thin descriptions, and ignore methodological difference.

Here we begin to make the case for our choice of methods by framing a case for how other methods have fallen short of success.

We set out to undertake an analysis and synthesis of findings from different studies using interpretive meta-ethnography. We had several objectives for undertaking such a task. First, we wanted to answer our own question, namely how does faculty thinking change as a result of moving from a more traditional teaching approach to an innovative educational approach? We believed that analysis of several studies could allow for interpretation beyond the scope of any single study. Second, we wanted to develop a framework for analyzing and synthesizing qualitative work. Third, we wanted to attempt the meta-ethnography, using our framework. Finally, we wanted to report findings we gathered through our analysis.	In this section, we outline our purpose of the study, making clear that we sought to inform disciplinary as well as methodological practices.
Our approach draws upon meta-ethnography as defined by Noblit and Hare (1988) but firmly locates the management and synthesis of findings in interpretivism. In practice, this meant not only that a transition and synthesis of one study into and across one another was required but also that, with the inclusion of an interpretive stance, data were reinterpreted. While such reinterpretation of data was important, we were also aware of the need to preserve the structure of the relationships between the concepts in the given studies. In order to be transparent about the work that we did, we provide in-depth descriptions of our research methods.	We intimate differences in our approach and classic approaches, while acknowledging the need to adhere to conventions, such as explicit descriptions of the search process.
Searching strategies In order to identify an initial pool of articles for possible inclusion in our study, we used standard search procedures, including using online search tools and hand searching. We also reviewed multiple bibliographies related to PBL, action learning and project-based learning. The actual data bases searched included the following: • Academic Search Elite (through EBSCO Host) • Allied and Alternative Medicine Database (AMED) • Applied Social Sciences Index and Abstracts (ASSIA) • Bath Information Data Service (BIDS) • Cumulated Index to Nursing and Allied Health Literature (CINAHL)	We used a variety of search approaches, relying heavily on electronic databases, making those as clear as possible so that others could repeat the search.

• The Cochrane Library (The Cochrane Database of systematic reviews, the Cochrane controlled trials register, the York database of abstracts of reviews of effectiveness) • Database of abstracts of reviews of effectiveness (DARE) • EMBASE (European version of MEDLINE) • ERIC International (contains a cluster of education databases) • MEDLINE (predominately American peer-reviewed journals) • National Research Library (NRR) • OTBibSys (includes occupational therapy, rehabilitation, education, healthcare delivery) • PsychLit (psychology and related disciplines) • Sociological Abstracts (sociology and related disciplines)	
In addition to standard searching methods, we engaged in several other approaches to identify potential studies, including scanning bibliographies of original and review articles for other suitable studies, hand searching, reviewing PBL Listservs and other relevant mailing lists, consulting with experts in the field and searching the Cochrane networks.	Due to differences in terms used by different researchers in different countries, electronic searching does not always locate all articles. For this reason, we also hand searched for articles, which yielded articles our electronic database search did not.
Our initial search yielded over 135 articles, edited collections and monographs. We knew that not all of these identified in our initial search would be relevant. Therefore, we had to select a method for determining which studies to include and which to exclude. Our primary guide for inclusion was topic area. We wanted to review and analyse studies that showed how undertaking problem-based learning, action learning, and project-based learning changed faculty thinking. However, we further narrowed articles found through using inclusion and exclusion criteria we deemed critical to our current work.	135 articles was too large a number for our methodology, and furthermore, not all of these articles were relevant. For these reasons, we knew we needed to narrow the scope of what articles we would include.

Table 1 indicates our predetermined list of criteria against which we reviewed each article to determine a decision about whether to include or not.

Table 1 Inclusion and exclusion criteria

Criteria	Include studies	Exclude studies
Topic	on faculty and problem-based learning, action learning, and project-based learning	on the training of faculty tutors
Question	About how faculty change as a result of problem-based learning, action learning, and project-based learning	of faculty perception of problem-based learning (i.e. like or dislike)
Date	conducted 1990 or later	conducted prior to 1990
Design	Using an interpretative qualitative design	using a quantitative design
Data	relying on in-depth participant interviews	relying on case studies, focus groups, observation, or content analysis

Here we provide our rationale for the selection criteria that we applied, to allow for greater transparency of process; criteria that were guided by our knowledge of PBL as well as of various qualitative approaches.

The rationale for using these criteria was threefold. First, we wanted to examine faculty experience specifically since we felt that this was an under-explored area in the field of active learning. In doing so, we found most of the studies related to PBL. Second, we believed that the studies on this topic area conducted prior to 1990 would not provide us with in-depth interpretative data or relevant cross-comparisons of studies since most of the studies until that time had been quantitative in nature. Furthermore, problem-based learning has changed in recent years, becoming more flexible in approach (Savin-Baden and Major 2004), so our selection was necessarily limited by fundamental changes in the approach; we thus chose studies in undertaken from 1990–2006. Third, we wanted to be able to actually compare study data in an interpretative way, and thus we believed that excluding studies that relied on case studies, focus groups, observation, or content analysis would enable us to concentrate on those studies in which it would be possible to reanalyze data. We therefore wanted to include studies grounded in the faculty experience.

Criteria for further evaluating the suitability of studies for inclusion

In determining which studies to include, we sought to stand against 'validity' as a position, which we suggest has led us to question and even meaningless practice in interpretive research. Instead we argue for 'honesties' (following Stronach, Corbin, Cmnamara, Stark, & Warne 2002) – a category that allows us to acknowledge that trust and truths are fragile whilst, at the same time,

In addition to setting criteria to allow inclusion of articles based on 'fit', we also determined that we needed to evaluate articles for 'quality' and thus set criteria that were important to us from a philosophical standpoint. We felt that if the authors had not demonstrated 'honesty', then there would be no way to judge the merit or worth of the study.

enables us to engage with the messiness and complexity of data interpretation in ways that really do reflect the lives of our participants (Savin-Baden & Fisher 2002). Honesties as a concept allows us to acknowledge not only the cyclical nature of 'truth', but also that the nature of honesties is defined by people and contexts and also helps us to avoid the prejudice *for* similarity and *against* difference in data interpretation. The conventional clustering of data and ways of 'ensuring' validity often result in a kind of formulae about how we 'do' validity and data interpretation. Instead we argue here for the presentation of difference and movement as well as more transparent approaches to validity claims that help us to engage with the way our participants often tell contradictory stories so that they are 'caught between stories, split between grounding narrative that offer(ed) different versions of a professional self along with tangential manifestations of a personal self' (Stronach *et al.* 2002, p.16). We believe there are a number of ways that we can engage with honesties in the research process and we began by using four, as identified by Savin-Baden and Fisher (2002):

1 Situating ourselves in relation to our participants
2 Voicing our mistakes

3 Situating ourselves in relation to the data

4 Taking a critical stance toward research

These methods for establishing honesties have been used as the basis of an evaluation instrument that was developed and used by Savin-Baden and Major (2004) to identify studies that reflected these values. We further revised these criteria to reflect our research approach of interpretive meta-ethnography, as demonstrated in Table 2.

Table 2 is the predetermined criteria against which we considered each study for credibility.

Table 2. Instrument for evaluating studies suitable for interpretive meta-ethnography

	0	1	2	3
	No Mention	Some Mention	Good Mention	Extensive Mention
Researcher(s) situated in relation to participants				
Mistakes voiced				
Researcher(s) situated in relation to the data				
Researcher(s) take a critical stance towards research				
Participant involvement in data interpretation				
Study theoretically situated				
Different versions of participants' identities acknowledged				

Selecting articles rated 2 or 3 in at least five of our seven categories allowed us to develop a pool of articles that we could reanalyze and reinterpret. However, this approach even further limited the number of potential articles.	As we realized that few, if any, articles would meet all of our criteria, we set a minimum standard for inclusion.
Studies selected Our selection of studies for inclusion was small. We found six articles that met our criteria for inclusion and that passed our evaluation. Interestingly, although our search reviewed articles from around the world, three studies were set in the US, and three were set in the UK. In some ways, we were disappointed with the low numbers, in particular because four of the six were written by authors of this article. We recognized the questions that including such a high percentage of articles that we had written would create for some, but adhering to our methodology and determined to be rigorous in our approach to 'honesties', we determined to proceed. The six works in our study are as follows: Savin-Baden 2000; Major & Palmer 2002; Major & Palmer 2006; Savin-Baden 2003; Wilkie 2004; Foord-May 2006. Since meta-ethnography is a new area and we had few guides about how to proceed we were not entirely sure how we were going to accomplish it; thus, starting small had the advantage of allowing us more opportunity to explore the ideas and methodological approaches.	Here, we acknowledged a small sample, in large part for the sake of reviewers, but we argued for the importance of retaining the methodological principles. We also situated the study as an exploratory one, from a methodological standpoint.

Summary of the studies used

Our purpose in conducting this study was to move beyond mere inductive comparison in ways that may just have provided an overview of the issues that emerged from each study. Before we present findings, though, we provide a summary of each of the studies which allows us later to demonstrate how our analysis moved beyond summary. The six studies used are described below and summarized in Table 3.

The first study we analyzed and interpreted was Savin-Baden (2000). This study was conducted over four years and examined the expectations and experiences of academic staff and students in different professional and educational environments, namely mechanical engineering, nursing, automotive design, and social work, who were involved in using problem-based learning. This study used both narrative approaches and new paradigm research. The findings illustrated that academic staff and students experienced disjunction in relation to three different 'stances'. These comprise the notions of Personal stance, Pedagogical stance and Interactional stance. Together the three stances encapsulate a holistic view of learner experience; a model termed 'Dimensions of Learner Experience'. The findings suggested that 'Dimensions of Learner Experience' offered a framework for understanding experiences of PBL while also asserting that learning through PBL may prompt reality construction and transformation in academic staff and students' past, present, and future learning.

We did not include a summary of the studies excluded, primarily because of space limitations of the journal (we were well over the length of articles they tend to publish even without a summary of excluded studies). However, we note that describing excluded studies can be useful to readers, since it gives them a clearer understanding of the field.

Here we summarized the context and methodologies of the studies we included, which was complemented by the graphic presentation that allows for easy comparison in Table 3. While this text is quite descriptive, it does illustrate to the readers the types of studies we used and illustrated textually how they met the inclusion criteria.

The second study (Major and Palmer 2002) took place at a private university in the south eastern United States that had been involved in a campus-wide project to improve teaching by implementing PBL. The research was undertaken with a group of 31 faculty members. Drawing on qualitative methods that involved data collection through 1:1 in-depth interviews, the authors describe several significant aspects of faculty pedagogical content knowledge. They believe that faculty knowledge is an iterative process by which faculty blend their knowledge of teaching and learning to enhance student-learning outcomes.

The third study (Major & Palmer 2006) draws from the research pool of the 31 faculty members involved in the grant-funded project to implement PBL across the university. This study examined the process of transforming faculty knowledge through in-depth face-to-face interviews. Researchers found that faculty existing knowledge and the institutional intervention influenced new knowledge of faculty roles, student roles, disciplinary structures and pedagogy brought about by adopting PBL. Communicating new knowledge solidified the transformation.

The fourth study (Savin-Baden 2003) was undertaken in a new School of Nursing and Midwifery at a UK university. The research was undertaken with a group of over 20 academic staff using collaborative and narrative inquiry because it allowed the research to be exploratory and reflexive. Data were collected through 1 to 1 in-depth interviews, informal discussions, email discussion and post interview reflections. In the early phase of data collection tutors spoke of their transitions from lecturer to facilitator using a variety of metaphors, but over the course of the study there was a considerable shift from their early perceptions and experiences to those they held later when they had become more accustomed to facilitating PBL teams. The shifts made by academic staff were perceived by them to be related to the students shifting from critical thinking to critique and thus they became facilitators of knowledge acquisition and understanding, rather than givers of knowledge. Thus although tutor stances did influence their overarching approach as facilitators, what seemed to be pivotal was the way in which they 'positioned' or 'placed' themselves.

The fifth study (Wilkie 2004) explored the espoused and actual conceptions of facilitation adopted by a group of nursing lecturers on an undergraduate nursing programme in the UK that utilized PBL. The research followed a group of 18 nursing lecturers over a three-year period as they implemented PBL within a three-year Diploma of Higher Education in Nursing programme. The research design was situated within a constructivist interpretivist paradigm. The constructivist approach is concerned with understanding and reconstructing, rather than explaining or predicting. Findings indicated four approaches to facilitation; however, the approaches were neither fixed nor hierarchical but were time and context dependent in relation to factors associated with students, with the PBL material or in response to changes in the facilitators themselves.

The final study (Foord-May 2006) examined faculty experience of the implementation of PBL in a physiotherapy programme. Basic qualitative interview methods were used to understanding faculty perspectives and data were collected. The study relied on semi-structured interviews with seven faculty. Data were analyzed using the constant comparative method and nine themes emerged that related to faculty perceptions of change and the required support for the implementation of an innovation such as PBL.

(note: in our exclusion and inclusion criteria for selecting articles, we excluded case studies because they tend to use multiple data sources (as advocated by Jensen and Rogers 2001; Merriam 1998; Yin 2002a, b), and thus in general, case study approaches often do not yield data that can be reanalyzed. Although Foord-May describes her methods as 'case study', she uses the term to refer to qualitative data that relies upon in-depth participant interviews; therefore, we did not exclude it from our study)

Table 3 provides a graphic comparison of the studies included so that the reader can easily note similarities and differences and identify any gaps in the information available

Table 3 Faculty perceptions of innovative experiences of learning

Methods, Perceptions and Concepts	Savin-Baden (2000)	Major and Palmer (2002)	Major and Palmer (2006)	Savin-Baden (2003)	Wilkie (2004)	Foord-May (2006)
Sample	22 academic staff	31 faculty	31 faculty	20 academic staff	18 academic staff	7 faculty
Setting	Four departments in four UK Universities	Private University in the US	Private University in the US	Faculty in UK University	Faculty in UK University	Department in US University
Methods	New paradigm research and narrative inquiry	Narrative inquiry	Narrative inquiry	Narrative and collaborative inquiry	Constructivist interpretivist paradigm	Qualitative inquiry
Data collection	Semi-structured interviews	Semi-structured interview	Semi structured interview	In-depth interviews, email discussions	Semi-structured interviews, audio taping of seminars	Semi-structured interviews; focus groups
Notion of validity	Trustworthiness and reflexivity	Trustworthiness and reflexivity	Trustworthiness and reflexivity	Trustworthiness and reflexivity	Trustworthiness and reflexivity	Participant validation
Positioning of researcher	Inquirer and reflexive learner	Inquirers and Insider/ outsider	Inquirers and Insider/outsider	Co-inquirer	Co-inquirer	Inquirer and researcher
Themes and concepts	Disjunction causes faculty change in pedagogical stance	Faculty knowledge of students is fundamentally altered with adoption of PBL	Faculty knowledge of discipline and pedagogy is altered with PBL and ultimately expressed differently	Pedagogical stance affects positioning of faculty in PBL environments	Facilitator approaches are affected by conceptions of learning	Support for faculty is vital for effective change management

Analysis, synthesis, and interpretation

The difficulty with analysis and synthesis in this kind of study is reflected by those that have already undertaken this kind of meta-ethnography. For example, suggestions by Britten *et al.* (2002) and Jones (2004) were compelling but seemed to lack an interpretive stance. Britten *et al.* throughout the course of the exemplar systematically decontextualized the studies, privileged some themes and issues over others, and tended to thin thick description, possibly in order to present their findings in an accessible tabulated format. Yet the original argument for meta-ethnography (Noblit & Hare 1988) is that through interpretation and by acknowledging the positions of the researchers as interpretivists, it is possible to recover the social and theoretical context of the research and thus reveal further noteworthy findings.	We believed it important to acknowledge the challenges of the method, while indicating that the benefits outweigh them. It was also important to illustrate the methodological differences between analysis, synthesis and interpretation.
We analyzed data by interpretative comparison and inductive analysis. Rather than just starting with raw data, we began with predetermined themes and descriptions that the original authors had chosen to include. Indeed, it is unusual in meta-ethnography to reinterpret the original data, and although we had access to much of this, we chose to stay as close as possible to methods used successfully by others (see for example Dixon-Woods, Agarwal, Jones, Young, & Sutton 2005; Mays, Pope, & Popay 2005; Smith, Pope, and Botha 2005). In practice this meant that not only were data compared and re-interpreted across the studies but also metaphors, ideas, concepts, and contexts were revisited in order to review how the initial findings had been contextualized and presented.	We cited some of the early efforts to use meta-synthesis; many works have been published since we initially developed this paper, which we cite throughout the text of this book.

In practice this meant that both of us: 1 Read the studies carefully and examined the relationship between them to determine common themes 2 Synthesized data and discussed the synthesizing in order to gain second-order interpretations 3 Developed third-order interpretations that added something that went beyond the mere comparisons of the findings of all the studies.	We used a three part process that amounted to analysis, synthesis and interpretation of data.
In order to share our findings, we believed that it was not necessary to preserve the structure of relationships between the concepts within each study; however, as data were interpreted interactively, reusing some themes might prove useful in some instances. Thus, although several themes crossed studies and some themes were relabelled to account for differences between the studies, we stayed as true as possible to the original themes in terms of subtextual comparison. Because we believed that forcing all data into common themes results in questionable research practices, though, we retained issues that diverged, pointing out differences.	We described the way that we adopted and adapted some themes, while acknowledging that some did not 'fit', which we highlighted further in the text.
Findings The findings presented in this section emerged in attempting to answer the research question: how does faculty thinking change as a result of moving from a more traditional teaching approach to an innovative educational approach? Undertaking such a study meant that new knowledge was brought to bear on existing material in terms of examining the impact of the discipline on the pedagogy of both PBL and faculty experience. Furthermore, it also raised questions about how tensions between professional demands for competency and academic demands for criticality are resolved and the degree of willingness amongst faculty to adopt a particular pedagogy, in this case, PBL. However, an issue that was particularly evident, which emerged because of specifically undertaking the interpretive meta-ethnography was the constellation of changes required by faculty in order to engage with both implementing PBL and developing a new and evolving role as facilitator.	We developed a narrative from the third order themes we discovered, selecting a 'narrative logic' as the organizational structure. While we found six cross-study themes, four of these seemed more prevalent, thus they formed the structure of the narrative, while we treated the remaining two as sub-themes that ran throughout the over-arching four themes.

Yet simultaneously faculty were not always entirely aware of the impact of the changes on their own academic identities and even departmental and institutional identity. Nevertheless four cross-data themes emerged, which were: 1 Changes in role perception 2 Changed perspectives about the nature of authority and control 3 Shifts in views about the nature of disciplinary knowledge 4 Changes in perception about the nature of teaching and learning **Changes in role perception** Several changes in perception of faculty roles were evident in all studies. Those changes are related below.	Theme 1 corresponded to the third order theme of 'change in teacher role'.
From lecturer to facilitator Faculty in all the studies described initial transitions from lecturer to facilitator. To begin with, they saw themselves as novice facilitators whose role it was to control and direct the team, fill in the gaps in the students' knowledge base, and ensure that the course content was covered. One of the US faculty members, Greg, changed his approach in introductory level biology courses as a part of a departmental move towards PBL. While in the early stages of his reformation, Greg described relinquishing more authoritative positions to assume positions as facilitator or guide: The course went from probably 75 to 80% lecture … and then it completely flipped… the biggest change that occurred there is that you remove yourself from the position of being the sole deliverer of information and being the lecturer who stands in front and dispenses, and you really have to give up and sacrifice your control over the class in that way.	This sub-theme appeared in some of the original articles, so we adopted it rather than creating a new term. We did not make distinctions between the studies using citational information, as few of the studies using this methodology make such distinctions (an exception is Major 2010). We did, however, note a difference in the voices of the UK staff and the US staff,

so we tended to identify articles by geographic origins to provide additional context.

We used thick description in the form of quotations from the original articles to support our interpretations.

So not walking in prepared to deliver a lecture, I should not say not being prepared, but not expecting to deliver it and having the pieces of the problem that you want them to work on is a very different mindset each time you go in the classroom.

Even though Greg espoused a change in role, there is evidence of his filling the gaps for the students in ways that he believed was important: 'what you want them to work on'. While this was not the case for all faculty members, it was the case for the majority of those in the early stages of transition. With more experience they began to shift, and later Greg began to move toward a more of a guide role, acknowledging that most of his work is done during the summer when he was not on contract; his work then involved developing problems and identifying potential resources.

Faculty in all studies seemed to have an awakening as they gained more experience with the facilitator role. A faculty member from the US, Ella, stated:

I would say, that, as a teacher, it's very rewarding to see people learn and be able to do things on their own, that you facilitated their learning as opposed to having them just memorize and say, Ella said, so I'm going to do it Ella's way because Ella thinks this, not that. It's much more; it's like the proverb, you can teach someone how to fish and they can fish for a lifetime rather than feed them for a day. I find that very rewarding and exciting to watch them grow and be successful.

Similarly, Lilly, a UK lecturer, said:

It [PBL]'s about getting them [students] to think for themselves. To look at the triggers and think 'What do I need to know about this, what should I learn?' It is not about telling them, keeping quiet.

Simon, a UK tutor was involved in multiple forms of teaching and learning. He had been given the overall remit of implementing curriculum change toward PBL, and at the same time, was implementing technological learning. His background in mental health nursing led him to believe that working and learning through a variety of approaches was useful, and he had assumed that as a facilitator he would not be particularly directive:

I didn't think for a minute that my normal teaching style was going to be okay as a problem-based learning facilitator, but I thought like many others do, that I do a lot of those things anyway. I ask a lot of questions, but it isn't until you actually think about being a facilitator, it's not just about asking questions, it's about the type of questions that you ask. And are the questions that you ask sufficiently open and non-directive to allow your students to think about issues and to find direction for themselves? So that I think I was just surprised about how much of a change was required of me.

Simon realized that he needed to change his style in order to offer students more autonomy; he saw the shift he needed to make as the difference between directing and guiding. He acknowledged that he was often directive and needed to change his position in relation to the students so that he no longer felt he needed to provide students with a lot of information and was able to leave them to discover information for themselves.

Changes in perspectives about the nature of authority and control

Although academic staff stances in all studies influenced their overarching approaches as facilitators, what seemed to be pivotal was the way in which they 'positioned' or 'placed' themselves. Thus in this sense the notion of how tutors positioned themselves does not displace their pedagogical stance (Savin-Baden 2000), but rather overlays it. This theme comprised three sub themes,

Theme 2 of the narrative corresponded with our third order theme 'Shifts in views about learning environment/context and the nature of authority and control', with sub themes related to environment and context outlined in the following sections.

His perception of himself as not being directive does not square with 'putting on my nursing lecturer's hat' so that he could supply students with the practical knowledge he felt they needed. Repositioning for control here is seen in the values that Jack demonstrated in practice – he no longer wanted students to challenge the *status quo*, instead he wanted to ensure they were heading in the right direction and had acquired the right knowledge, skill and capabilities for practice. While this view in many ways is ethically sound and illustrates a desire to equip students well, such narrow facilitation practices are likely to prevent the possibility of developing the kinds of criticality he first espoused.

Faculty in the US tended to maintain even more control than those in the UK. Eloise, for example, who had discovered PBL herself and was using it in isolation from colleagues who did not use it at all adopted the approach in her introduction to education courses. While espousing the idea that she wanted to give control, her explanation of how this might be done suggested otherwise:

> What you want to cover, your destination, your goal, how you are going to get from Point A to B, and that has to remain the teacher's responsibility. The student doesn't have that expertise. But then the students' responsibility is to actually assemble those little guides along the way, get involved and do it.

In similar fashion, Marilyn, a pharmacy professor also claimed ownership of the learning and ultimately became a judge of the final value of the learning:

> Because with PBL you really have to decide what do you fundamentally want them to learn. And then what else they learn is really driven by them. And you have to decide how much of that is necessary and how much of it is extra and you hope they learn more.

all related to the notion of repositioning: repositioned to maintain control, repositioned to offer control and repositioned to relinquish control.

(Re)positioned to maintain control

Jack, a UK academic staff member, presented a picture of one whose values would initially seem to be repositioned but in fact the values in use illustrated a need to be in control of knowledge. Initially Jack argued that there was not enough flexibility within the nursing profession about what was to be valued and what counted as knowledge. He found it difficult to discuss PBL separately from his perspective on life and saw students engaging with learning as a life-process. He believed that students should, at every level of the program, be encouraged to question the knowledge, skills and ethical principles laid before them and to challenge the *status quo*. Thus Jack saw knowledge as something that was to be challenged and explored not only within the framework of the university, but also within practice, and across the culture of practice and higher education. His main concern was that the underlying principles of PBL were only being contained within components of the curriculum. However, a year later it became apparent that the views he had first spoken of were not espoused in the practices of PBL he adopted:

I try not to be directive although at times I say to the group, I think I'm taking my problem-based learning hat off for a few minutes is that okay, so they know the difference, now I'm putting on my nursing lecturer's hat and I will throw something out to them which is possibly a gaping hole in their argument and they should have identified it, so I will give it to them. Now go back and play with that ball, and I'll put that problem-based learning hat back on again. I think I'm that kind of facilitator, not directive, give them a long lead, do a lot of listening, try to play the game they want to play as long as they look at the objectives of the problem-based learning, and they are heading in that direction.

This and the three following sub themes appeared in one of our original articles and encompassed many similar themes in the remaining five.

(Re)positioned to offer control

Tutors also repositioned themselves in order to promote self-direction in students. However, although they offered control, sometimes they did not then give it to the students, and at other times students chose not to take that control even though it was offered. Neil, for example, was a lecturer in mental health and adult nursing in the UK who had worked in several institutional settings and said he enjoyed the move to PBL. To begin with, he felt that this was just because it was a change in teaching style, but later he valued it in terms of the challenges it brought for him personally and pedagogically. He explained:

I don't know how to put it, you don't see yourself as a teacher, you don't see yourself as a lecturer, yours is a different role. You have expertise in the area that you work, but it's not teaching, you are not really here to do teaching, you are here teaching outside the frame. I find it rewarding in the way that you know you see the student moving on, you see the student buzzing, you know, but in terms of me giving, that's one thing I don't know, what do I give?

In a later interview Neil still did not see himself as a teacher, but his position had moved toward seeing himself more in partnership with the students in the learning process:

... and quite a few times I have seen myself almost as the student, you know, I was learning from them and I wouldn't say that it was something that I found surprising, you know, because the way problem-based learning is... and you know I would be picking up from them and sometimes afterwards ask them for copies of the pieces of work they have presented which actually made them aware that you know, its their work.

Neil repositioned himself both in relation to the teaching approach and in relation to the students. He saw himself as an enabler of learning and a learner.

In similar fashion, some of the US faculty expressed similar notions of themselves as learners alongside their students. A business faculty member, Katie, explained her experience like this:

> There's nothing hard to understand about marketing, so they understand the subject at one level already because they've been a target of marketing communications for their entire lives. And so I really expect to learn from them and how they view what's happening to them in a marketing environment, how they would act as a marketing manager, you know, how do they perceive a particular situation. It's relevant to me as an instructor but also as a researcher to see how they think. So, I tend to expect that I will learn as much from them as they would learn from me.

(Re)positioned to relinquish control

Faculty in this sub theme sought to encourage both collaborative and dialogic learning so that students developed their ability to use dialogue, discussion and prior experience to enhance their learning. Tutors' concerns here were in relinquishing control to students so that autonomy was not just espoused but was played out in practice. Sally, a UK tutor, was a member of the academic staff who had been working with postgraduate students for many years. She had described herself as a non-directive facilitator, but the accounts she offered of what she did when facilitating her PBL team indicated the dilemmas of being displaced in this context. Initially she felt at odds with this approach to learning because she believed that being a good teacher meant she needed to ensure that students did not have gaps in their knowledge base.

For her, failing to point out the gaps was irresponsible and she was not prepared to wait to let students discover the gaps for themselves in the weeks ahead, in case they missed them and then that would be her fault (not theirs). Yet some 2 years later she was repositioned as someone who wanted to relinquish control and be a responsible facilitator, but also she felt her role as a tutor was one where directing students was no longer her place. She explained:

We still have arguments about this as PBL facilitators, you still hear people saying I have done all this preparation for this trigger, it took me hours to do this, and I am still saying to them, why? You are not doing these triggers, your group is doing this trigger. Your job is there to try and help them see the way that they've got to go with it, and if you're preparing stuff it may not be what they need to know. So I would be saying to someone 'yes don't go and get the trigger out of the cupboard just as you walk into the class', you know... So I think be well prepared when you go into class, but only be prepared to facilitate the group, not be prepared to teach them what the trigger is telling them, and I think that that is really really important...

Kevin, a US faculty member who teaches special education courses had a similar experience of relinquishing control. He explained it as follows:

It was a big jump, because, you know, I think of myself as a want-to-be physician. I deal with all these physical problems with kids, and if I don't spend 3 hours lecturing about Down's syndrome. But then, you know, when you think about it, they'll remember that information to the mid-term or their next exam and then forget it. So I really had to let go – it was a control issue – of my didactic practices, of standing up there lecturing and you 'write this down, this is on the test', to letting go. That's fine.

Shifts in views about the nature of disciplinary knowledge

Faculty across the studies expressed new understandings of their disciplines. Simon explained his frustration with academic staff who believed that didactic teacher-centred approaches were the only way to produce good nurses, as they saw disciplinary knowledge as 'volume':

Well, the rationale underpinning problem-based learning was explained to these people and they were – and attempts were made to engage them in dialogue about the rationale and the principles behind an alternative way of delivering biological science material... The staff in that group operate on the belief that attendance at a lecture by a student equates with acquisition of that large body of knowledge, and they obviously believe that they imparting that large body of knowledge to the student equates with learning.

Faculty members in the US often reported perceiving their disciplines in new ways, particularly describing the complexities and challenges they experienced. As a professor of English explained:

I think that was a major shift for me as a teacher because I began to realize something about my discipline that I never realized before and that was the complexity of it. I created the problem not knowing what it was going to do, and then the first time I did it with students I started seeing all these questions coming up that even I had never thought before.

Designing PBL added to the depth of their knowledge in their content area, and frequently prompted changes in their ideas about how to teach the content of their discipline. The change in perspective frequently occurred in two ways, as a breaking down of artificial boundaries within the discipline and in breaking down barriers across disciplinary areas. Faculty comments also highlighted another important outcome of the course redesign process; rather than relying

Theme 3 corresponded with our third-order interpretation similarly titled 'Shifts in views about the nature of disciplinary knowledge'.

on textbooks for the organizational structure of a particular area of content, they began to see the walls within the discipline break down:

> That's why I'm using it so much. I have really started to learn the depth of my own discipline in a way that I had not understood. I haven't seen it before, as connected to other disciplines in ways that I haven't seen before, because my education, probably like yours, was so disciplined oriented. I studied literature and now I'm able to see what I do as a writer and what I do as a teacher and student of literature in just multiple ways. In seeing literature intersecting with science in my CP class, seeing literature intersecting with philosophy, so PBL, this is for the most selfish of reasons, I think, it has helped me be a better student and I have got to become a student again. That's why I'm excited about it.

Faculty were rejuvenated by a return to the role of learner that learning a new way of teaching required as they began to see new and different aspects of their own disciplines through recognizing connections with other disciplines.

Changes in perception about the nature of teaching and learning

While we identified many shared changes across the groups of faculty in the studies, they seemed to diverge in one area, and that is their perception of the nature and role of teaching. The US group tended to talk more about perceiving the importance of teaching in a new way than the UK group did. This could be due to basic differences in interview protocol, differences in academic staff development, or the difference in the emphasis that different institutions placed on this. It could also be because of the relative newness of the national attention to the 'scholarship of teaching' movement, espoused by Boyer (1990), Hutchings and Shulman (1999), and others, which have moved educators toward

Theme 4 corresponded with the third order theme with the similar title. This theme is where we saw the most divergence, which we pointed out here as well as in the narrative.

a national conversation about the importance of talking about teaching and disseminating the knowledge gained in the classroom. It might also be because of the impact of changes in teaching and learning in the UK in recent years and the introduction of postgraduate certificates in higher education for lecturing academic staff across the sector, which make teaching and learning part of an internal conversation.	
Teaching for understanding	We relabelled this and the following sub-themes because none of the themes from the original articles quite captured the ideas when viewing them altogether.
Faculty in the US began to see teaching as a rich activity, worthy of reflection, and investigation. As Nadene, a business professor described:	
It's made me very aware that that space or feeling or interaction or whatever it is has properties and qualities that I'm interested in researching and understanding theoretically. But there are days when it's more. It's more effective, it's more alive, because there's more exchange between me and the students, and I think that space is best created through active learning strategy …. That is not me teaching, but it's the class learning	Doing so illustrates the importance of being flexible about when and whether to use the primary themes from articles or whether to use new ones – we did both.
Spaces for learning offer faculty and students opportunities to examine their cultural context. The frameworks by which people live and operate may thus be challenged and transcended through the act of evaluating the world and themselves and even that very act of self-evaluation. Yet opportunities for such individual and corporate reflection can only emerge within curricula where the belief in reflection is not only espoused but also are undertaken in practice. Such belief can only emerge from the premise that independent inquiry and reflection upon one's life-world is worthwhile and to be valued within professions and academic institutions.	

Teaching as shared practice

Faculty in the US began to see teaching as something that could be articulated and shared with others. One professor suggested that he shared his course information and teaching ideas as similar to building upon one another's research ideas:

> You know we've got to start sharing this stuff, not keep it locked up and hidden away, afraid somebody's going to steal it. And part of it, like our portfolio project, is part taking teaching away, opening up the door and sharing what's going on in there, and that's where I sort of think we've got to go next, is to find ways so we're not all reinventing the wheel.

Faculty also realized that they could communicate with one another around issues of teaching in a more complex and productive manner, and while unusual at first, conversations about teaching and learning became regular fare.

Teaching as research

In more formal ways, faculty members communicated their new knowledge to their peers, such as workshops, conference presentations, journal articles, course portfolios, and new research projects. Thus, we saw that faculty had begun to think of pedagogy and teaching in their fields as scholarship.

As one US faculty member, who also had administrative responsibilities for his programme, put it:

> I was trying to explain to the staff the kind of research that I expected to come out of this program, cause I did say 'I don't want this to be just about teaching. I think there ought

to be this nice give and take between what we do in the classroom, what we do in the way of our research and scholarship'. And …[many faculty] have English degrees and their scholarship probably has been in the area of criticism and interpretation, which doesn't always relate real directly to a course like [this one]. And, so I wanted them to think about their work with the students as something that had a research angle to it. I thought if I'm going to say that, then I need to show that. So I took a student paper from this course, before we did the problem-based learning and set up the assignment to doing that, and then I took one from a student who had written a paper with the problem-based learning assignment and compared those two to say 'What happened differently in these two assignments?' …. But as I analyzed those two, I think they began to see the differences that were going on in them and how problem-based learning has a real effect on the outcome, in this case the students' piece of writing.

Faculty who changed their teaching methods also had practical reasons for the dissemination of their work. In short, they started to believe that in order for teaching to be rewarded, it had to become more public. As David, an untenured geography professor in the US, explained:

So, yeah, and for myself, I made the decision that if I'm going to do this, I've got to make it count, so I've written a couple of things. I've done presentations at conferences, I've done some consulting and all of that kind of stuff, and I figure if I'm going to be spending time on this rather than doing something else, I've got to have something to show for it. So yeah, professionally it has made a difference that way.

Discussion

Faculty in these studies re-examined their understanding of their roles as the lecturer, of their students' role as learners, of the structures of their disciplines and of their views of teaching. As participants reflected on their experiences, the combined effect of time, resources, support for risk-taking, and collegial discussion presented an unusual gateway for the transformation of their pedagogical stances, knowledge, and practice.

Teacher knowledge is a complex concept that includes knowledge of learners, knowledge of subject matter, previous experiences, and ideas about pedagogical practice and contextual cues in a dynamic iterative process that can be supported and encouraged through institutional intervention. Like meaningful learning, faculty learning about pedagogical content knowledge begins by connecting to what the learner already knows, produces a transformation and then continues to be modified as the learner encounters additional related experiences. While faculty in the studies received varying levels of institutional support, very few seemed to receive support or guidance in ways of managing transitions in the change process; further research, particularly case study research, could examine this question more closely.

Many of the faculty found self-management a complex task, while they were simultaneously helping students to manage their own transitions toward learning approaches that few had previously encountered. Although this was the case for the majority of faculty in this study, there continued to be others who were not prepared to make shifts of any kind. However, facilitators valued support from each other and many facilitators commented that the support of other facilitators had been a major influence in adjusting to and developing PBL. Yet at the same time they experienced 'the complexities and tensions inherent in two major sources of identity, one local, visible and tangible, the other cosmopolitan, largely invisible and disembedded' (Henkel 2000: 19), in short their department and their university. Thus the institution in which academics are located and position themselves ensure that knowledge production and transmission occurs in particular and acceptable ways to both the profession and the academics, while also sustaining their professional identities as academics.

In our discussion, we highlighted the main themes and returned to a discussion of related literature. This was in order to recontextualize the study and provide a space from which to develop the ideas and discoveries that emerged from the findings

What we found particularly useful about the research method we selected, meta ethnography, was the examination of issues, methods and concepts across the studies. Interpretive meta-ethnography such as this affords us an opportunity not only to compare studies and the themes identified by the authors but also to construct an (always contestable) interpretation. Here, we were able to move beyond themes to second and even third levels of interpretation. What the synthesis added was the importance of facilitating change in academic identities and in confronting issues of power and control in innovative approaches to learning.

Since the methodology was relatively new and relatively rare in our field, we included thoughts about the benefits of the approach.

Table 4 is a direct representation of the themes that we found and illustrates the complex nature of the approach, in that all findings appear in the table as if they were of equal importance, which they were not, as we indicated in the narrative.

Table 4 Cross-Study Analysis, Synthesis, and Interpretation of Data

Overarching concepts/ themes	Second order interpretations (i.e. analysis and comparisons)	Third order interpretations (data and conceptual interpretations)
Conception of knowledge	Challenging view of epistemology	Shifts in views about the nature of disciplinary knowledge
View of pedagogical stance	Engaging with issues of power and control	Shifts in views about learning environment/context and the nature of authority and control
Realization of need for change	Self-evaluating and determining the cost and risk of change	Reflection on professional responsibility as a teacher; identification of need for change in personal and academic positioning
Understanding of teaching and learning	Identifying new ways of instructional development	Change in perception about complexity of the new teaching approach
Perception of role	Questioning teacher identity	Change in teacher role
Perception of others	Seeing new roles for students	Recognition of students as partners in learning, with administrators and students

	Given our intended audience of researchers, our recommendations were primarily geared toward making suggestions for future research.
Future research, we believe, should be conducted on how faculty decisions to radically alter their approaches to teaching and learning alters their understanding of their roles, their students' roles, the discipline and the approach in question (whether PBL, project-based learning or some other). We argue that such future inquiry will allow for a greater understanding of faculty pedagogical knowledge, a greater acknowledgement of the changed and changing nature of 'discipline', an exploration of 'disciplinary drift', and greater focus on the scholarship that is inherent in changing approaches to teaching and learning. In addition, future attempts at meta-ethnography could draw upon what we have done here, extending and challenging our work. Different criteria for inclusion and exclusion and different methods of evaluating students based upon different philosophical stances in relation to research can only add to the existing body of research, directing and developing new ways to *know* and *understand*. We would welcome an ongoing discussion in the literature about whether such approaches are useful, and if so, how they might best be conducted. ## Conclusion This complex synthesis, analysis and interpretation of six studies advances the field of knowledge and it aids our growth as researchers. We believe that if we do not begin to compare findings and situate our studies within a larger interpretive context, we may indeed find ourselves to be a part of an endangered species. However, we also felt a sense of dis-ease with our method. We wondered at times whether we should even have even attempted such an approach. Is it an example of everything we as researchers fight so hard against: an objectivist, reductionist approach that denies and belies collaboration with participants? We present this research in the hope of beginning a conversation about moving forward and understanding that only time and effort will prove whether such an approach helps, hurts or does both.	While tying the conclusion directly to the findings was important, we also believed it critical to comment on the experience of using this methodology and acknowledging both its value and shortcomings.

We did not mark citations included in the synthesis with an asterisk, as the journal's style guidelines did not indicate that we should. Had we been using APA format, however, we probably would have done so.

References

Albanese, M. A., & Mitchell, S. (1993). Problem-based learning: A review of literature on its outcomes and implementation issues. Academic Medicine: Journal of the Association of American Medical Colleges, 68(1), 52–81.

Boyer, E. (1990). Scholarship reconsidered: Priorities of the professorate. Special report. Princeton, NJ: The Carnegie Foundation for the Advancement of Teaching.

Britten, N., Campbell, R., Pope, C., Donovan, J., Morgan, M., & Pill, R. (2002). Using meta ethnography to synthesise qualitative research: A worked example. Journal of Health Services Research Policy, 7(4), 209–215.

Dahlgren, M. A., Castensson, R., & Dahlgren, L. O. (1998). The PBL from the teachers' perspective: conceptions of the tutor's role within problem based learning. Higher Education, 36(4), 437–447.

Delanty, G. (2001). Challenging knowledge. The university in the knowledge society. Buckingham: Open University Press/SRHE.

Dixon-Wood, M., Agarwal, S., Jones, D., Young, B., & Sutton, A. (2005). Synthesizing qualitative and quantitative evidence: A review of possible methods. Journal of Health Services Research and Policy, 10(1), 45–53.

Foord-May, L. (2006). A faculty's experience in changing instructional methods in a professional physical therapy education programme. Physical Therapy, 86(2), 223–235.

Henkel, M. (2000). Academic identities and policy change in higher education. London: Jessica Kingsley Publishers.

Hutchings, P., & Schulman, L. (1999). The scholarship of teaching: New elaborations, new developments. Change, 31(5), 10–15.

Jenkins A., & Zetter, R. (2003). Linking teaching and research in departments. York: LTSN Generic Center.

Jensen, J., & Rodgers, R. (2001). Cumulating the intellectual gold of case study research. Public Administration Review, 61(2), 236–246.

Jones, K. (2004). Mission drift in qualitative research, or moving toward a systematic review of qualitative studies, moving back to a more systematic narrative review. The Qualitative Report, 9(1), 95–112. Retrieved (14 November 2005), from http://www.nova.edu/ssss/QR/QR9-1/jones.pdf

Major, C. H., & Palmer, B. (2002). Faculty knowledge of influences on student learning. The Peabody Journal of Education, 77(3), 137–161.

Major, C. H., & Palmer, B. (2006). Reshaping teaching and learning: Changing faculty pedagogical content knowledge. Higher Education, 51(4), 619–647.

Martin, E., Prosser, M., Trigwell, K., Ramsden, P., & Benjamin, J. (2000). What university teachers teach and how they teach it. Instructional Science, 28, 387–412.

Mays, N., Pope, C., & Popay, J. (2005). Systemically reviewing qualitative and quantitative evidence to inform management and policy-making in the health field. Journal of Health Services Research and Policy, 10(1), 1–20.

Merriam, S. B. (1998). Qualitative research and case study applications in education. San Francisco, CA: Jossey-Bass Publishers.

Noblit, G. W., & Hare, R. D. (1988). Meta-ethnography: Synthesizing qualitative studies. Newbury Park, CA: Sage.

Savin-Baden, M. (2000). Problem-based learning in higher education: Untold stories. Buckingham: Open University Press/SRHE.

Savin-Baden, M. (2003). Facilitating problem-based learning: Illuminating perspectives. Buckingham: Open University Press/SRHE.

Savin-Baden, M., & Fisher, A. (2002). Negotiating "honesties" in the research process. British Journal of Occupational Therapy, 65(4), 191–193.

Savin-Baden, M., & Major, C. H. (2004). Foundations of problem-based learning. Maidenhead: SRHE/Open University Press.

Shulman, L. (1986). Those who understand: Knowledge growth in teaching. Educational Researcher, 15(2), 4–14.

Shulman, L. (1987). Knowledge and teaching: Foundations of the new reform. Harvard Educational Review, 57(1), 1–22.

Smith, L. K., Pope, C., & Botha, J. L. (2005). Patients' help-seeking experiences and delay in cancer presentation: A qualitative synthesis. The Lancet, 366, 825–831.

Stronach, I., Corbin, B., McNamara, O., Stark, S., & Warne, T. (2002). Towards an uncertain politics of professionalism: Teacher and nurse identities in flux. Journal of Educational Policy, 17(1), 109–138.

Vernon, D. A., & Blake, R. L. (1993). Does problem-based learning work? A meta-analysis of evaluative research. Academic Medicine, 68(7), 550–563.

Wilkie, K. (2004). Becoming facilitative: shifts in lecturers' approaches to facilitating problem-based learning. In M. Savin-Baden & K. Wilkie (Eds.), Challenging research in problem-based learning. Maidenhead: SRHE and Open University Press.

Yin R. (2002a). Case study research (3rd ed.). Thousand Oaks, CA: Sage Publications.

Yin R. (2002b). Applications of case study research (2nd ed.). Thousand Oaks, CA: Sage Publications.

Bibliography

Texts about qualitative synthesis

Anagnostou, Y. (2006) 'Meta-ethnography in the age of "popular folklore"', *Journal of American Folklore*, 119(474): 381–412.

Atkins, S., Lewin, S., Smith, H., Engel, M., Fretheim, A. and Volmink, J. (2008) 'Conducting a meta-ethnography of qualitative literature: Lessons learnt', *BMC Medical Research Methodology*, 8(21). Retrieved January 9, 2009, from http://www. biomedcentral.com/1471-2288/8/21.

Banning, J. (n.d.) 'Ecological triangulation: an approach for qualitative meta-synthesis. What Works for Youth with Disabilities Project', U.S. Department of Education. Retrieved January 22, 2009, from http://mycahs.colostate.edu/James.H.Banning/ PDFs/Ecological%20Triangualtion.pdf.

Bland, C. J., Meurer, L. N. and Maldonado, G. (1995) 'Systematic approach to conducting nonstatistical meta-analysis of research literature', *Academic Medicine*, 70(7): 642–653.

Bondas, T. (2007) 'Challenges in approaching metasynthesis research', *Qualitative Health Research*, 17(1): 113–121.

Bondas, T. and Hall, E. O. C. (2007) 'A decade of metasynthesis research in health sciences: A meta-method study', *International Journal of Qualitative Studies on Health and Well-Being*, 2(2): 101–113.

Booth, A. (2006) '"Brimful of STARLITE": toward standards for reporting literature searches', *Journal of the Medical Library Association*, 94(4): 421–429, e205.

Britten, N., Campbell, R., Pope, C., Donovan, J., Morgan, M. and Pill, R. (2002) 'Using meta ethnography to synthesise qualitative research: a worked example', *Journal of Health Services Research Policy*, 7(4): 209–215.

Campbell, R., Pound, P., Pope, C., Britten, N., Pill, R. and Morgan, M. (2003) 'Evaluating Meta-ethnography: A synthesis of qualitative research on lay experiences of diabetes and diabetes care', *Social Science and Medicine*, 56(4): 671–684.

Carroll, S. M. (2004) 'Nonvocal ventilated patients' perceptions of being understood', *Western Journal of Nursing Research*, 26(1): 85–103. February 5, 2009, from http://wjn. sagepub.com/cgi/reprint/26/1/85

Coffman, M. J. (2004) 'Cultural caring in nursing practice: A meta-synthesis of qualitative research', *Journal of Cultural Diversity*, 11(3): 100–109.

Conn, V. S., Valentine, J. C., Cooper, H. M. and Rantz, M. (2003) 'Grey literature in meta-analyses', *Nursing Research*, 52: 256–261.

Crismore, A. (1985) 'The case for a rhetorical perspective on learning from texts: Exploring metadiscourse' (Tech. Rep. No. 342).

Davies, P. (2000) 'The relevance of systematic reviews to educational policy and practice', *Oxford Review of Education*, 26(3–4): 365–378.

Denyer, D. and Tranfield, D. (2006) 'Using qualitative research synthesis to build an actionable knowledge base', *Management Decision*, 44(2): 213–227.

Dixon-Woods, M., Agarwal, S., Jones, D., Young, B. and Sutton, A. (2005) 'Synthesising qualitative and quantitative evidence: a review of possible methods', *Journal of Health Services Research & Policy*, 10(1): 45–53.

Dixon-Woods, M., Bonas, S., Booth, A., Jones, D., Miller, T., Sutton, A. J., Shaw, R. L., Smith, J. A. and Young, B. (2006) 'How can systematic reviews incorporate qualitative research? A critical perspective', *Qualitative Research*, 6(1): 27–44.

Dixon-Woods, M., Cavers, D., Agarwal, S., Annandale, E., Arthur, A., Harvey. J., Hsu, R., Katbamna, S., Olsen, R., Smith, L., Riley, R. and Sutton, A. J. (2006) 'Conducting a critical interpretive synthesis of the literature on access to healthcare by vulnerable groups', *BMC Medical Research Methodology*, 6(35): 1–13.

Dixon-Woods, M., Booth, A. and Sutton, A. J. (2007) 'Synthesizing qualitative research: a review of published reports', *Qualitative Research*, 7(3): 375–422. Retrieved February 5, 2009, from http://qrj.sagepub.com/cgi/reprint/7/3/375.

Dixon-Woods, M., Fitzpatrick, R. and Roberts, K. (2008) 'Including qualitative research in systematic reviews: opportunities and problems', *Journal of Evaluation in Clinical Practice*, 7(2): 125–133.

Dixon-Woods, M., Shaw, R. L., Agarwal, S. and Smith, J. A. (2004) 'The problem of appraising qualitative research', *Quality & Safety in Health Care*, 13(3): 223–225.

Downe, S. (2008) 'Meta-synthesis: a guide to knitting smoke', *Evidence Based Midwifery*, 6(1): 4–8.

Doyle, L. H. (2003) 'Synthesis through meta-ethnography: Paradoxes, enhancements, and possibilities', *Qualitative Research*, 3(3): 321–344.

Estabrooks, C. A., Field, P. A. and Morse, J. M. (1994) 'Aggregating qualitative findings: An approach to theory development', *Qualitative Health Research*, 4: 503–511.

Evans, D. and Pearson, A. (2001) 'Systematic reviews of qualitative research', *Clinical Effectiveness of Nursing*, 5(3): 111–119.

Finfgeld, D. L. (2003) 'Metasynthesis: The state of the art-so far', *Qualitative Health Research*, 13(7): 893–904.

Flemming, K. (2007) 'The synthesis of qualitative research and evidence-based nursing', *Evidence-Based Nursing*, 10(3): 68–71.

Forbes, A. and Griffiths, P. (2002) 'Methodological strategies for the identification and synthesis of "evidence" to support decision-making in relation to complex healthcare systems and practices', *Nursing Inquiry*, 9(3): 141–155.

Goldsmith, M. R., Bankhead, C. R. and Austoker, J. (2007) 'Synthesizing quantitative and qualitative research in evidence-based patient information', *Journal of Epidemiology & Community Health*, 61(3): 272–270.

Gough, D. and Elbourne, D. (2002) 'Systematic research synthesis to inform policy, practice, and democratic debate', *Social Policy & Society*, 1(3): 225–236.

Hammersley, M. (2002) 'Systematic or Unsystematic, is that the Question? Some reflections on the science, art, and politics of reviewing research evidence', *Text of a talk given to the Public Health Evidence Steering Group of the Health Development Agency, October,*

2002. Retrieved February 2, 2009, from http://www.nice.org.uk/niceMedia/pdf/sys_unsys_phesg_hammersley.pdf.

Hammersley. M. and Foster, P. (1998) 'A review of reviews: structure and function in reviews of educational research', *British Educational Research Journal*, 24(5): 609–628.

Harden, A. and James, T. (2005) 'Methodological issues in combining diverse study types in systematic reviews', *International Journal of Social Research Methodology*, 8(3): 257–271.

Harden, A., Garcia, J., Oliver, S., Rees, R., Shepherd, J., Brunton, G. and Oakley, A. (2004) 'Applying systematic review methods to studies of people's views: an example from public health service', *Journal of Epidemiology and Community Health*, 58(9): 794–800.

Heaton, J. (2004) *Reworking qualitative data*. London: Sage.

HM Treasury (2003) 'What do we already know? Harnessing Existing Research', *The magenta book: guidance notes for policy evaluation and analysis*. Retrieved January 28, 2009, from http://www.gsr.gov.uk/downloads/magenta_book/Chap_2_Magenta.pdf.

Hossler, D. and Scalese-Love, P. (1989) 'Grounded meta-analysis: A guide for research syntheses', *Review of Higher Education*, 13(1): 1–28.

Huang, Y. and Wilkinson, I. F. (n.d.) 'Interpreting Interpretive Research'. Retrieved January 29, 2009, from http://www.sobmedia.commerce.otago.ac.nz/asp/anzmac07/anzmacCD/papers/YHuang_2.pdf.

Hundersmarck, S. (in press) 'Is synthesizing qualitative research possible? A study about the process of synthesizing qualitative studies in the field of education using three alternative forms of synthesis', *The Qualitative Report*. Retrieved February 4, 2009, from https://www.msu.edu/~mkennedy/TQQT/Reports/HundersmarckInPress.pdf.

Jensen, J. and Rodgers, R. (2001) 'Cumulating the intellectual gold of case study research', *Public Administration Review*, 61(2): 236–246.

Johnson, M. (2001) 'Systematic reviews of qualitative research', *Clinical Effectiveness in Nursing*, 5(3): 118.

Jones, K. (2004) 'Mission drift in qualitative research, or moving toward a systematic review of qualitative studies, moving back to a more systematic narrative review', *The Qualitative Report*, 9(1): 95–112. Retrieved [14 November 2005], from http://www.nova.edu/ssss/QR/QR9-1/jones.pdf.

Levin, R. and Feldman, H. R. (2006) *Teaching evidence-based practice in nursing. A guide for academic and clinical settings*. New York: Springer.

Light, R. J. and Pillemar, D. B. (1982) 'Numbers and narrative: combining their strengths in research reviews', *Harvard Educational Review*, 52(1): 1–26.

Lomas, J. (2005) 'Using research to inform healthcare managers' and policy makers' questions: from summative to interpretive synthesis', *Healthcare Policy/ Politiques de Santé*, 1(1): 55–71.

Mays, N., Pope, C. and Popay, J. (2005) 'Systemically reviewing qualitative and quantitative evidence to inform management and policy-making in the health field', *Journal of Health Services Research and Policy*, 10(1): 1–20.

Mays, N., Roberts, E. and Popay, J. (2001) 'Synthesizing research evidence', in Naomi Fulop (ed.) *Studying the organization and delivery of health services*. Routledge, pp. 188–220.

McCormick, J., Rodney, P. and Varcoe, C. (2003) 'Reinterpretations across studies: An approach to meta-analysis', *Qualitative Health Research*, 13(7): 933–944.

Morse, J. M. (2001) 'Qualitative verification: Building evidence by extending basic findings', in J. Morse, J. Swanson, and A. Kuzel (eds.) *The Nature of Qualitative Evidence*. Thousand Oaks, CA: Sage, pp. 203–220.

Nicholas, D. B., Globerman, J., Antle, B. J., McNeill, T. and Lach, L. M. (2006) 'Processes of metastudy: A study of psychosocial adaptation to childhood chronic health conditions', *International Journal of Qualitative Methods*, 5(1): Article 5. Retrieved January 28, 2009, from http://www.ualberta.ca/~iiqm/backissues/5_1/html/nicholas.htm.

Noblit, G. W. and Hare, R. D. (1983) 'Meta-ethnography: Issues in the synthesis and replication of qualitative research', *Paper presented at the Annual Meeting of the American Educational Research Association (67th, Montreal, Quebec, April 11–15, 1983)*. Retrieved January 9, 2009, from http://eric.ed.gov/ERICWebPortal/custom/portlets/recordDetails/detailmini.jsp?_nfpb=true&_&ERICExtSearch_SearchValue_0=ED231853&ERICExtSearch_SearchType_0=no&accno=ED231853. (ERIC# ED231853)

Noblit, G. W. and Hare, R. D. (1988) *Meta-ethnography: Synthesizing Qualitative Studies*. Newbury Park, CA: Sage.

Palacios, W. R. (2007) 'Suspending 'fieldwork': A meta-ethnography of illicit drug-using behavior', *Paper presented at the annual meeting of the AMERICAN SOCIETY OF CRIMINOLOGY, Atlanta Marriott Marquis, Atlanta, Georgia*. Retrieved January 26, 2009, from http://www.allacademic.com/meta/p_mla_apa_research_citation/2/0/0/8/0/p200800_index.html.

Paterson, B. L. and Thorne, S. (2003) 'The potential of metasynthesis for nursing care effectiveness research', *Canadian Journal of Nursing Research*, 35(3): 39–43.

Paterson, B. L., Thorne, S. E., Canam, C. and Jillings, C. (2001) *Meta-study of Qualitative Health Research. A Practical Guide to Meta-analysis and Meta-synthesis*. Thousand Oaks, CA: Sage.

Paterson, B. L., Canam, C., Joachim, G. and Thorne, S. (2003) 'Embedded assumptions in qualitative studies of fatigue', *Western Journal of Nursing Research*, 25(2): 119–133.

Pearson, A. (2004) 'Balancing the evidence: Incorporation the synthesis of qualitative data into systematic reviews', *JBI Reports*, 2(2): 45–64.

Pope, C. Mays, N., Popay, J. (2007) *Synthesizing Qualitative and Quantitative Health Evidence: A Guide to Methods*, London: Open University Press.

Potts, A., Boler, M., Hicks, D., Doolittle, P., Ariew, S., Cachaper, C., Carico, K. and Prickett, R. (2004) 'Qualitative meta-analysis for social justice: The creation of an on-line diversity resources database', in C. Crawford *et al.* (eds.) *Proceedings of Society for Information Technology and Teacher Education International Conference 2004*. Chesapeake, VA: AACE, pp. 832–836.

Rantala, K. and Wellstrom, E. (2001) 'Qualitative comparative analysis and a hermeneutic approach to interview data', *International Journal of Social Research Methodology*, 4(2): 87–100.

Reis, S., Hermoni, D., Van-Raalte, R., Dahan, R. and Borkan, J. (2007) 'Aggregation of qualitative studies – from theory to practice: patient priorities and family medicine/general practice evaluations', *Patient Education and Counseling*, 65(2): 214–222.

Rice, E. H. (2002) 'The collaboration process in professional development schools: Results of a meta-ethnography, 1990–1998', *Journal of Teacher Education*, 53(1): 55–67.

Rist, R. (1990) 'Meta-ethnography', *Educational Studies*, 21: 364–367.

Ritzer, G. (1992) 'Metatheorizing in sociology: Explaining the coming of age', in G. Ritzer (Ed.) *Metatheorizing* (pp. 7–26). Newbury Park, CA: Sage.

Rossman, G. B. (1993) 'Building explanations across case studies: A framework for synthesis', *Colorado Univ., Boulder. School of Education.* Retrieved February 16, 2009, from http://www.eric.ed.gov/ERICDocs/data/ericdocs2sql/content_storage_01/0000019b/80/16/20/7a.pdf.

Rousseau, D. M., Manning, J. and Denyer, D. (2008) 'Evidence in management and organizational science: Assembling the field's full weight of scientific knowledge through synthesis', *The Academy of Management Annals,* 2: 475–515.

Sandelowski, M. (2004) 'Using qualitative research', *Qualitative Health Research,* 14(10): 1366–1386.

Sandelowski, M. (2006) '"Meta-Jeopardy": The crisis of representation in qualitative metasynthesis', *Nursing Outlook,* 54(1): 10–16.

Sandelowski, M. and Barroso, J. (2002a) 'Finding the findings in qualitative studies', *Image: Journal of Nursing Scholarship,* 34(3): 213–220.

Sandelowski, M. and Barroso, J. (2002b) 'Reading qualitative studies', *International Journal of Qualitative Methods,* 1(1) Article 5. Retrieved September 1, 2006, from http://www.ualberta.ca/~ijqm/.

Sandelowski, M. and Barroso, J. (2003a) 'Classifying the findings in qualitative studies', *Qualitative Health Research,* 3(7): 905–923.

Sandelowski, M. and Barroso, J. (2003b) 'Creating meta-summaries of qualitative findings', *Nursing Research,* 52(4): 226–231.

Sandelowski, M. and Barroso, J. (2007) *Handbook for Synthesizing Qualitative Research.* New York: Springer.

Sandelowski, M., Barroso J. and Voils C. I. (2007) 'Using qualitative metasummary to synthesize qualitative and quantitative descriptive findings', *Research in Nursing Health,* 30(1): 99–111.

Sandelowski, M., Docherty, S. and Emden, C. (1997) 'Qualitative metasynthesis: Issues and techniques', *Research in Nursing and Health,* 20(4): 365–371.

Schreiber, R., Crooks, D. and Stern, P. N. (1989) 'Qualitative metaanalysis', in J. M. Morse (ed.) *Qualitative nursing research: A contemporary dialogue.* London: Sage. pp. 311–327.

Sherwood, G. D. (1999) 'Meta-synthesis: Merging qualitative studies to develop nursing knowledge', *International Journal for Human Caring,* 3(1): 37–42.

Suri, H. (1999) 'A methodically inclusive model for research synthesis', *Paper presented at the Annual Meeting of the Australian Association of Research in Education (AARE), Melbourne, 29 November–2 December, 1999.* Retrieved February 5, 2009, from http://www.aare.edu.au/99pap/sur99673.htm.

Suri, H. and Clark, D. (1998) 'Revisiting methods of literature synthesis', *A paper presented at the Annual Meeting of the Australian Association of Research in Education (AARE), Adelaid, 20 November–3 December, 1998.* Retrieved February 16, 2009, from http://www.eric.ed.gov/ERICDocs/data/ericdocs2sql/content_storage_01/0000019b/80/1a/0e/75.pdf.

Suri, H. and Clarke, D. (2009) 'Advancements in research synthesis methods: From a methodologically inclusive perspective', *Review of Educational Research,* 79(1): 395–430.

The Joanna Briggs Institute (2007) The Joanna Briggs Institute Approach to Evidence-Based Practice. The Joanna Briggs Institute. Accessed 27 May, 2007, from http://www.joannabriggs.edu.au/pdf/about/Approach.pdf.

Thomas, J. and Harden, A. (2008) 'Methods for the thematic synthesis of qualitative research in systematic reviews', *BMC Medical Research Methodology*, 8: 45.

Thompson, C. (2001) 'Systematic reviews of qualitative research', *Clinical Effectiveness in Nursing*, 5(3): 117–118.

Thorne, S. (1994) 'Secondary analysis in qualitative research: Issues and implications', In J. M. Morse (ed.) *Critical issues in qualitative research methods*. London: Sage. pp. 263–279.

Thorne, S. (1998) 'Ethical and representational issues in qualitative secondary analysis', *Qualitative Health Research*, 8(4): 547–555.

Thorne, S., Jensen, L., Kearney, M. H., Noblit, G. and Sandelowski, M. (2004) 'Qualitative metasynthesis: Reflections on methodological orientation and ideological agenda', *Qualitative Health Research*, 14(10): 1342–1365.

Tickle-Degnen, L. (1999) 'Organizing, evaluating, and using evidence in occupational therapy practice', *American Journal of Occupational Therapy*, 53(5): 537–539.

Troman, G. and Jeffrey, B. (2007) 'Qualitative data analysis in cross-cultural projects', *Comparative Education*, 43(4): 511–525.

Walsh, D. and Downe, S. (2005) 'Meta-synthesis method for qualitative research: a literature review', *Journal of Advanced Nursing*, 50(2): 204–211.

Walsh, D. and Downe, S. (2006) 'Appraising the quality of qualitative research', *Midwifery*, 22(2): 108–119.

Weed, M. (2005a) '"Meta Interpretation": A method for interpretive synthesis of qualitative research', *Forum Qualitative Sozialforschung*, 6(1): Art. 37.

Weed, M. (2005b) 'Research synthesis in sports management: Dealing with "chaos in the brickyard,"' *European Sports Management Quarterly*, 5(1): 77–90.

Weed, M. (2006) 'Interpretive qualitative synthesis in the sport and exercise sciences: The meta-interpretation approach', *European Journal of Sport Science*, 6(2): 127–139.

Whittemore, R. (2005) 'Combining evidence in nursing research: methods and implications', *Nursing Research*, 54(1): 56–62.

Zhao, S. (1991) 'Metatheory, metamethod, meta-data-analysis: What, why, and how?', *Sociological Perspectives*, 34(8): 377–390.

Zimmer, L. (2006) 'Qualitative meta-synthesis: a question of dialoguing with texts', *Journal of Advanced Nursing*, 53(3): 311–318.

Research articles employing qualitative synthesis

Aagaard, H. and Hall, E. (2008) 'Mothers' experiences of having a preterm infant in the neonatal care unit: A meta-synthesis', *Journal of Pediatric Nursing*, 23(3): e26–e36.

Al-Janabi, H., Coast, J. and Flynn, T. N. (2008) 'What do people value when they provide unpaid care for an older person? A meta-ethnography with interview follow-up', *Social Science & Medicine*, 67(1): 111–121.

Apprey, M. (2005) 'A formal grounded theory on the ethics of transfer in conflict resolution', Research paper: CASE Weatherhead School of Management. Retrieved January 23, 2009, from http://weatherhead.case.edu/edm/archive/files/year2/Apprey--revised%20SYRP1%209-9-05.pdf.

Apprey, M. (2007) 'An attempt to create an ethic of transfer after conflict resolution in fractured communities: a modified formal grounded theory shaped by meta-ethnography', *Psychotherapy and Politics International*, 5(2): 130–152.

Attree, P. (2005a) 'Low-income mothers, nutrition, and health: a systematic review of qualitative evidence', *Maternal & Child Nutrition*, 1(4): 227–240.

Attree, P. (2005b) 'Parenting support in the context of poverty: a meta-synthesis of the qualitative evidence', *Health & Social Care in the Community*, 13(4): 330–337.

Attree, P. (2004a) 'Growing up in disadvantage: a systematic review of the qualitative evidence', *Child: Care, Health, and Development*, 30(6): 679–689.

Attree, P. (2004b) *Parenting in Disadvantage: A Meta-synthesis of the Qualitative Evidence*. Lancaster: Lancaster University, Institute for Health Research. Retrieved January 30, 2009, from, http://www.lancs.ac.uk/fass/ihr/publications/pamattree/parentingindisadvantage.pdf.

Attree, P. (2006b) 'The social costs of child poverty: a systematic review of the qualitative evidence', *Children & Society*, 20(1): 54–66.

Au, W. (2007) 'High-stakes testing and curricular control: A qualitative meta-synthesis', *Educational Researcher*, 36(5): 258–267.

Bair, C. R. (1999) 'Meta-synthesis', *Paper presented at the Annual Meeting of the Association for the Study of Higher Education (24th, San Antonio, TX, November 18–21, 1999)* ERIC # ED437866. Retrieved January 29, 2009, from http://eric.ed.gov/ERICDocs/data/ericdocs2sql/content_storage_01/0000019b/80/16/09/44.pdf.

Bair, C. R. and Haworth, J. G. (2005) 'Doctoral student attrition and persistence: a meta-synthesis of research', in J.C. Smart (ed.) *Higher Education: Handbook of Theory and Research* (vol. 19). Springer: Netherlands. pp. 481–534.

Bales, S. and Wang, P. (2006) 'Consolidating user-relevance criteria: A meta-ethnography of empirical studies', *Proceedings of the American Society of Information Science and Technology*, 42(1).

Barroso, J. and Powell-Cope, G. M. (2000) 'Metasynthesis of qualitative research on living with HIV infection', *Qualitative Health Research*, 10(3): 340–53.

Barroso, J. and Sandelowski, M. (2003) 'Sample reporting in qualitative studies of women with HIV infection', *Field Methods*, 15(4): 386–404.

Barroso, J., Gollop, C.J., Sandelowski, M., Meynell, J., Pearce, P. F. and Collonis, L.J. (2003) 'The challenges of searching for and retrieving qualitative studies', *Western Journal of Nursing Research*, 25(2): 153–178.

Beck, C. (2002a) 'Mothering multiples: A metasynthesis of qualitative research', *MCN: American Journal of Maternal Child Nursing*, 27(4): 214–221.

Beck, C. (2002b) 'Postpartum depression: A metasynthesis', *Qualitative Health Research*, 12(4): 453–472.

Beck, C. T. (2001) 'Caring within nursing education: a metasynthesis', *Journal of Nursing Education*, 40(3): 101–109.

Beck, C. T. (2003) 'Seeing the forest for the trees: A qualitative synthesis project', *Journal of Nursing Education*, 42(7): 318–321.

Berry, B. (1985) 'Understanding Teacher Supply and Demand in the Southeast: A Synthesis of Qualitative Research to Aid Effective Policy Making', Occasional Papers in Educational Policy Analysis. Paper No. 420. Southeastern Regional Council for Educational Improvement, Research Triangle Park, NC.

Clemmens, D. (2003) 'Adolescent motherhood: a meta-synthesis of qualitative studies', *The American Journal of Maternal/Child Nursing*, 28(2): 93–99.

Denny, E. and Kahn, K. (2006) 'Systematic reviews of qualitative evidence: What are the experiences of women with endometriosis?', *Journal of Obstetrics & Gynecology*, 26(6): 501–506.

DeWitt-Brinks, D. and Rhodes, S. C. (1992) *Listening Instruction: A Qualitative Meta-Analysis of Twenty-Four Selected Studies* (Rep. No. Clearinghouse: CS507954), U.S.; Michigan.

Dixon-Woods, M., Cavers, D., Agarwal, S., Annandale, E. *et al.* (2006) 'Conducting a critical interpretive synthesis of the literature on access to healthcare by vulnerable groups', *BMC Medical Research Methodology*, 6(35): 1–13.

Dixon-Woods, M., Seale, C., Young, B., Findlay, M. and Heney, D. (2003) 'Representing childhood cancer: account from newspapers and parents', *Sociology of Health & Wellness*, 25(2): 143–164.

Douglas, A. C., Mills, J. E., Niang, M., Stepchenkova, S., Byun, S., Ruffini, C. *et al.* (2008) 'Internet addiction: meta-synthesis of qualitative research for the decade 1996–2006', *Computers in Human Behavior*, 24(6): 3027–3044.

Downe, S., Simpson, L. and Trafford, K. (2006) 'Expert intrapartum maternity care: a meta-synthesis', *Journal of Advanced Nursing*, 57(2): 127–140.

Duggan, F. and Banwell, L. (2004) 'Constructing a model of effective information dissemination in a crisis', *Information Research*, 9(3). Retrieved January 21, 2009, from http://informationr.net/ir/9-3/paper178.html.

Dundon, E. (2006) 'Adolescent depression: A meta-synthesis', *Journal of Pediatric Health Care*, 20(6): 384–392.

Edwards, M., Davies, M., Edwards, A. (2009). 'What are the external influences on information exchange and shared decision-making in healthcare consultations: A meta-synthesis of the literature', *Patient Education and Counseling*, 75(1): 37–52.

Emery, J., Watson, E., Rose, P. and Andermann, A. (1999) 'A systematic review of the literature exploring the role of primary care in genetic services', *Family Practice*, 16(4): 426–445.

Emslie, C. (2005) 'Women, men, and coronary heart disease: a review of the qualitative literature', *Journal of Advanced Nursing*, 51(4): 382–395.

Espindola, S. R. and Blay, S. L. (2006) 'Bulimia and binge eating disorder: Systematic review and meta-synthesis', Revista de Psiquiatria do Rio Grande do Sul, 28(3). Retrieved February 4, 2009, from http://www.scielo.br/scielo.php?pid=S0101-81082006000300006&script=sci_arttext&tlng=en.

Evans, D. and FitzGerald, M. (2002) 'The experience of physical restraint: A systematic review of qualitative research', *Contemporary Nurse*, 13(2–3): 126–135.

Feder, G. S., Hutson, M., Ramsay, J. and Taket, A. R. (2006) 'Women exposed to intimate partner violence: Expectations and experiences when they encounter health care professionals: A meta-analysis of qualitative studies', *Archives of Internal Medicine*, 166(1): 22–37.

Finfgeld, D. L. (1999) 'Courage as a process of pushing beyond the struggle', *Qualitative Health Research*, 9(6): 803–814.

Foster, S. (1998) 'Communication as social engagement: implications for interactions between deaf and hearing persons', *Scandinavian Audiology*, 27(4), Supplement 49: 116–124.

Garside, R., Britten, N. and Stein, K. (2008) 'The experience of heavy menstrual bleeding: a systematic review and meta-ethnography of qualitative studies', *Journal of Advanced Nursing*, 63(6): 550–562.

Gately, C., Rogers, A., Kirk, S. and McNally, R. (2008) 'Integration of devices into long-term condition management: A synthesis of qualitative studies', *Chronic Illness*, 4(2): 135–148.

Glasmeier, A. K. and Farrigan, T. (2005) 'Understanding community forestry: a qualitative meta-study of the study, the process, and its potential for poverty alleviation in the United States case', *Geographic Journal*, 171(1): 56–69.

Goodman, J. H. (2006) 'Becoming an involved father or an infant', *Journal Obstetric, Gynecologic, and Neonatal Nursing*, 34(2): 190–200.

Gustafsson, C., Asp, M. and Fagerberg, I. (2007) 'Reflective practice in nursing care: Embedded assumptions in qualitative studies', *International Journal of Nursing Practice*, 13(3): 151–160.

Hager, W. and Hasselhorn, M. (1998) 'The effectiveness of the cognitive training for children from a differential perspective: A meta-evaluation', *Learning and Instruction* 8(9): 411–438.

Hammell, K. W. (2007) 'Experience of rehabilitation following spinal cord injury: a meta-synthesis of qualitative findings', *Spinal Cord*, 45(4): 260–274.

Hammell, K. W. (2007) 'Quality of life after spinal cord injury: a meta-synthesis of qualitative findings', *Spinal Cord*, 45(2): 124–139.

Harvey, D. J. (2007) 'Understanding Australian rural women's ways of achieving health and wellbeing: A meta-synthesis of the literature,' *Rural and Remote Health*, 7: 823. Retrieved May 26, 2009 from http://www.rrh.org.au/publishedarticles/article_print_823.pdf

Hidalgo, K. M. (2006) 'Embodiment of hospice nurses: A meta-synthesis of qualitative studies', *Journal of Hospice & Palliative Nursing*, 8(3): 137–146.

Hildingh, C., Fridlund, B. and Lidell, E. (2007) 'Women's experiences of recovery after myocardial infarction: A meta-synthesis', *Heart & Lung: The Journal of Acute and Critical Care*, 36(6): 410–417.

Himam, F. (2002) 'Inventing the future: A meta-ethnographic analysis towards understanding the process of individual and organizational adaptive strategies to change', *ETD collection for University of Nebraska - Lincoln*. Paper AAI3055275. Retrieved January 28, 2009, fromhttp://digitalcommons.unl.edu/dissertations/AAI3055275.

Howard, A. F., Balneaves, L. G. and Bottorff, J. L. (2007) 'Ethnocultural women's experiences of breast cancer: A qualitative meta-study', *Cancer Nursing*, 30(4): E27–E35.

Jensen, L. A. and Allen, M. N. (1994) 'A synthesis of qualitative research on wellness-illness', *Qualitative Health Research*, 4(4): 349–369.

Jensen, L. A. and Allen, M. N. (1996) 'Meta-synthesis of qualitative findings', *Qualitative Health Research*, 6(4): 553–560.

Kane, G. A., Wood, V. A. and Barlow, J. (2007) 'Parenting programmes: a systematic review and synthesis of qualitative research', *Child: Care, Health, and Development*, 33(6): 784–793.

Kasworm, C. E. (2000) 'Adult Undergraduates in Higher Education: A Review of Past Research Perspectives', *Review of Educational Research*, 60(3): 345–372.

Kearney, M. (1998) 'Truthful self-nurturing: A grounded formal theory of women's addiction recovery', *Qualitative Health Research*, 8(4): 495–512.

Kennedy, H. P., Rousseau, A. L. and Low, L. K. (2003) 'An exploratory meta-synthesis of midwifery practice in the United States', *Midwifery*, 19(3): 203–214.

Khan, N., Bower, P. and Roger, A. (2007) 'Guided self-help in primary care mental health: Meta-synthesis of qualitative studies of patient experience', *The British Journal of Psychiatry*, 191: 206–211.

Larun, L. and Malterud, K. (2007) 'Identity and coping experiences in Chronic Fatigue Syndrome: A synthesis of qualitative studies', *Patient Education and Counseling*, 69(1–3): 20–28.

Major, C. (2010) 'Do virtual professors dream of electric students? College faculty experiences with online distance education', *Teachers College Record*, 112(8).

Malpass, A., Shaw, A., Sharp, D., Walter, F., Feder, G., Ridd, M. and Kessler, D. (2009) '"Medication career" or "Moral career"? Two sides of managing antidepressants: A meta-ethnography of patient's experience of antidepressants', *Social Science & Medicine*, 68(1): 154–168.

Martin, D., O'Neill, J., Randall, D. and Rouncefield, D. (2007) '"How can I help you?" Call centers, classification work, and coordination', *Computer Supported Cooperative Work*, 16(3): 231–264.

Martisen, B., Paterson, B., Harder I. and Biering Sørensen, F. (2007) 'The nature of feeding completely dependent persons: A meta-ethnography', *International Journal of Qualitative Studies on Health and Well-being*, 2(4): 208–216. Retrieved from January 21, 2009, from http://www.informaworld.com/smpp/content~content=a77740208 6~db=all.

McClean, S. and Shaw, A. (2005) 'From schism to continuum? The problematic relationship between expert and lay knowledge – an exploratory conceptual synthesis of two qualitative studies', *Qualitative Health Research*, 15(6): 729–749.

McDermott, E. and Graham, H. (2005) 'Resilient young mothering: Social inequalities, late modernity and the 'problem' of 'teenage' motherhood', *Journal of Youth Studies*, 8(1): 59–79.

Meadows-Oliver, M. (2004) 'Mothering in public: a meta-synthesis of homeless women with children living in shelters', *Journal of Specialists in Pediatric Nursing*, 8(4): 130–136.

Meadows-Oliver, M. (2007) 'Homeless adolescent mothers: A meta-synthesis of their life experiences', *Journal of Pediatric Medicine*, 21(5): 340–349.

Metcalfe, A., Coad, J., Plumridge, P. M., Gill, P. and Farndon, P. (2008) 'Family communication between children and their parents about inherited genetic conditions: a meta-synthesis of research', *European Journal of Human Genetics*, 16(10): 1193–1200.

Mills, E. J., Montori, V., Ross, C.P., Shea, B., Wilson, K. and Guyatt, G. (2005) 'Systematically reviewing qualitative studies compliments survey design: an exploratory study of barriers to pediatric immunizations', *Journal of Clinical Epidemiology*, 58(11): 1101–1108.

Mills, E., Jadad, A. R., Ross, C. and Wilson, K. (2005) 'Systematic review of qualitative studies exploring parental beliefs and attitudes toward childhood vaccination identifies common barriers to vaccination', *Journal of Clinical Epidemiology*, 58(11): 1081–1088.

Mills, E. J., Seely, D., Rachlis, B., Griffith, L., Wu, P., Wilson, K., Ellis, P. and Wright, J. R. (2006) 'Barriers to participation in clinical trials of cancer: a meta-analysis and systematic review of patient-reported factors', *The Lancet, Oncology*, 7(2): 141–148.

Mills, E., Wilson, K., Rachlis, B., Griffith, L., Wu, P., Guyatt, G. and Cooper, C. (2006) 'Barriers to participation in HIV drug trials: a systematic review', *The Lancet Infectious Diseases*, 6(1): 32–38.

Molony, S. L. (2007) 'A meta-synthesis of the meaning of home', *Paper presented to the 19th Annual Scientific Sessions of Eastern Nursing Research Society, in Providence, Rhode Island, April 12 to 14, 2007*.

Nelson, A. M. (2002) 'A meta-synthesis: mothering other-than-normal children', *Qualitative Health Research*, 12(4): 515–530.

Nelson, A. M. (2006a) 'A metasynthesis of qualitative breastfeeding studies', *Journal of Midwifery & Women's Health*, 51(2): e13–e20.

Nelson, A. M. (2006b) 'Transition to motherhood', *Journal of Obstetric, Gynecological, and Neonatal Nursing*, 32(4): 465–477.

Noyes, J. and Popay, J. (2007) 'Directly observed therapy and tuberculosis: How can a systematic review of qualitative research contribute to improving services? A qualitative meta-synthesis', *Journal of Advanced Nursing*, 57(3): 227–243.

O'Neill, T., Jinks, C. and Ong, B. N. (2007) 'Decision-making regarding total knee replacement surgery: a qualitative meta-synthesis', *BMC Health Services Research*, 10(7): 52.

Paterson, B. L. (2001) 'The shifting perspectives model of chronic illness', *Image: Journal of Nursing Scholarship*, 33(1): 21–26.

Paterson, B. L. (2004) 'The shifting perspectives model of chronic illness', *Journal of Nursing Scholarship*, 33(1): 21–26.

Paterson, B. L., Thorne, S. and Dewis, M. (2007) 'Adapting to and managing diabetes', *Journal of Nursing Scholarship*, 30(1): 57–62.

Pielstick, C. D. (1998) 'The transforming leader: a meta-ethnographic analysis', *Community College Review*, 26(3): 15–34.

Pound, P., Britten, N., Morgan, M., Yardley, L., Pope, C., Daker-White, G. and Campbell, R. (2005) 'Resisting medicines: a synthesis of qualitative studies of medicine taking', *Social Science & Medicine*, 61(1): 133–155.

Raffo, C. (2006) 'Disadvantaged young people accessing the new urban economies of the post-industrial city', *Journal of Education Policy*, 21(1): 75–94.

Rhodes, T. and Treloar, C. (2008) 'The social production of hepatitis C risk among injecting drug users: a qualitative synthesis', *Addiction*, 103(10): 1593–1603.

Roberts, K. A., Dixon-Woods, M., Fitzpatrick, R., Abrams, K. and Jones, D. (2002) 'Factors affecting uptake of childhood immunization: a Bayesian synthesis of qualitative and quantitative analysis', *The Lancet*, 360(9345): 1596–1599.

Sandelowski, M. and Barroso, J. (2003c) 'Motherhood in the context of maternal HIV infection', *Research in Nursing and Health*, 26(6): 470–482.

Sandelowski, M. and Barroso, J. (2003d) 'Toward a metasynthesis of qualitative findings on motherhood in HIV-positive women', *Research in Nursing and Health*, 26(2): 153–170.

Sandelowski, M. and Barroso, J. (2006) 'The travesty of choosing after postitive prenatal diagnosis', *Journal of Obstetric, Gynecologic, and Neonatal Nursing*, 34(3): 307–318.

Sandelowski, M. Voils, C. I. and Barroso, J. (2006) 'Comparability work and the management of difference in research synthesis', *Social Sciences & Medicine*, 64(1): 236–247.

Savin-Baden, M. and Major, C. H. (2007) 'Using interpretive meta-ethnography to explore the relationship between innovative approaches to learning and innovative methods of pedagogical research', *Higher Education,* 54(6): 833–852.

Savin-Baden, M. and Wilkie, M. (2004) 'Exploring the impact of discipline-based pedagogy on problem-based learning through interpretive meta ethnography', in M. Savin-Baden and K. Wilkie (eds) *Challenging Research in Problem-based Learning*. Maidenhead: Open University Press/SRHE.

Savin-Baden, M., Macfarlane, L. and Savin-Baden, J. (2007) 'Influencing thinking and practices about teaching and learning in higher education. An interpretive meta-ethnography', *Higher Education Academy* http://www.heacademy.ac.uk/projects/detail/lr_2007_savinbaden (Accessed 8 July 2008).

Savin-Baden, M., Macfarlane, L. and Savin-Baden, J. (2008) 'Learning spaces, agency and notions of improvement: Influencing thinking and practices about teaching and learning in higher education. An interpretive meta-ethnography', *London Review of Education*, 6(3): 211–229.

Scruggs, T. E., Mastropieri, M. A. and McDuffie, K. A. (2007) 'Co-teaching in inclusive classrooms: a metasynthesis of qualitative research', *Exceptional Children*. Retrieved January 12, 2009, from http://www.accessmylibrary.com/coms2/summary_0286-32297231_ITM.

Sherwood, G. D. (1997) 'Metasynthesis of qualitative analysis of caring', *Advances in Nursing Science*, 3(1): 32–42.

Siau, K. and Long, Y. (2005) 'Synthesizing e-government stage models: a meta-synthesis based on meta-ethnography approach', *Industrial Management & Data Systems*, 105(4): 443–458.

Sim, J. and Madden, S. (2008) 'Illness experience in fibromyalgia syndrome: A meta-synthesis of qualitative studies', *Social Science & Medicine*, 67(1): 57–67.

Skrla, L., Scott, J. and Benestante, J. J. (2001) 'Dangerous intersection: A meta-ethnographic study of gender, power, and politics in the public school superintend-ency', in C. C. Brunner and L. Bjork (eds.) *Advances in research and theories of school management and educational policy: The new superintendency*. Stamford, CT: JAI Press. pp. 115–131.

Smith, L. K., Pope, C. and Botha, J. L. (2005) 'Patients' help-seeking experiences and delay in cancer presentation: a qualitative synthesis', *The Lancet*, 366(9488): 825–831.

Stein, W. W. (2003) *Deconstructing Development in Peru: A meta-ethnography of the modernity project at Vicos*. New York: University Press of America.

Swartz, M. K. (2005) 'Parenting preterm infants: A meta-synthesis', *The American Journal of Maternal/Child Nursing*, 30(2): 115–120.

Thorne, S. and Paterson, B. (2002) 'Two decades of insider research: What we know and don't know about chronic illness experience', *Annual Review of Nursing Research*, 18: 3–25.

Thorne, S., Joachim, G., Paterson, B. and Canam, C. (2002) 'Influence of the research frame on qualitatively derived health science knowledge', *International Journal of Qualitative Methods*, 1(1) Article 1. Retrieved September 1, 2006, from http://www.ualberta.ca/~iiqm/backissues/1_1Final/html/thorneeng.html.

Thorne, S., Paterson, B., Acorn, S., Canam, C., Joachim, G. and Jillings, C. (2002) 'Chronic illness experience: Insights from a metastudy', *Qualitative Health Research*, 12(4): 437–452.

Tong, A., Lowe, A., Sainsbury, P. and Craig, J. (2008) 'Experiences of parents who have children with chronic kidney disease: a systematic review of qualitative studies', *PEDIATRICS*, 121(2): 349–360.

Varcoe, C., Rodney, P. and McCormick, J. (2003) 'Health care relationships in context: An analysis of three ethnographies', *Qualitative Health Research*, 13(7): 957–973.

Vermeire, E., Hearnshaw, H., Rätsep, A., Levasseur, G. *et al.* (2007) 'Obstacles to adherence in living with type-2 diabetes: An international qualitative study using meta-ethnography', *Primary Care Diabetes*, 1(1): 25–33.

Walter, F. M., Emery, J., Braithwaite, D. and Marteau, T. (2004) 'Lay understanding of familial risk of chronic diseases: a systematic review and synthesis of qualitative research', *Annals of Family Medicine*, 2: 583–594.

Wilson, K. and Amir, Z. (2008) 'Cancer and disability benefits: a synthesis of qualitative findings on advice and support', *Psycho-oncology*, 17(5): 421–429.

Xu, Y. (2007) 'Strangers in strange lands: A meta-synthesis of lived experiences of immigrant Asian nursing working in Western countries', *Advances in Nursing Science*, 30(3): 245–265.

Yager, R. E. (1982) 'Factors involved with qualitative synthesis: A new focus for research in science education', *Journal of Research in Science Technology*, 19(5): 337–350.

Yick, A. G. (2008) 'A meta-synthesis of qualitative findings on the role of spirituality and religiosity among culturally diverse domestic violence survivors', *Qualitative Health Research*, 18(9): 1289–1306.

Ypinazar, V. A., Margolis, S. A., Haswell-Elkins, M. and Tsey, K. (2007) 'Indigenous Australians' understandings regarding mental health and disorders', *Australian and New Zealand Journal of Psychiatry*, 41(6): 467–478.

Yu, D. S. F., Lee, D. T. F., Kwong, A. N. T., Thompson, D. R. and Woo, J. (2008) 'Living with chronic heart failure: a review of qualitative studies of older people', *Journal of Advanced Nursing*, 61(5): 474–483.

References

Aagaard, H. and Hall, E. (2008) 'Mothers' experiences of having a preterm infant in the neonatal care unit: A meta-synthesis', *Journal of Pediatric Nursing*, 23(3): e26–e36.

Armstrong, E. C. (1999) 'The well-built clinical question: The key to finding the best evidence efficiently', *Wisconsin Medical Journal*, 98(2): 25–28.

Attree, P. (2004a) 'Growing up in disadvantage: a systematic review of the qualitative evidence'. *Child: Care, Health, and Development*, 30(6): 679–689.

Attree, P. (2004b) *Parenting in Disadvantage: A Meta-synthesis of the Qualitative Evidence*, Lancaster: Lancaster University, Institute for Health Research. Retrieved January 30, 2009, from, http://www.lancs.ac.uk/fass/ihr/publications/pamattree/parentingindisadvantage.pdf.

Attree, P. (2005a) 'Low-income mothers, nutrition, and health: a systematic review of qualitative evidence', *Maternal & Child Nutrition*, 1(4): 227–240.

Attree, P. (2005b) 'Parenting support in the context of poverty: a meta-synthesis of the qualitative evidence', *Health & Social Care in the Community*, 13(4): 330–337.

Bailey, C. A. (1996) *A Guide to Field Research*. Thousand Oaks, CA: Pine Forge Press.

Bair, C. R. and Haworth, J. G. (2005) 'Doctoral student attrition and persistence: a meta-synthesis of research', in J.C. Smart (ed.) *Higher Education: Handbook of Theory and Research* (vol. 19). Springer: Netherlands. pp. 481–534.

Barroso, J., Gollop, C. J., Sandelowski, M., Meynell, J., Pearce, P. F. and Collonis, L. J. (2003) 'The challenges of searching for and retrieving qualitative studies', *Western Journal of Nursing Research*, 25(2): 153–178.

Beck, C. (2002a) 'Mothering multiples: A metasynthesis of qualitative research', *MCN: American Journal of Maternal Child Nursing*, 27(4): 214–221.

Beck, C. (2002b) 'Postpartum depression: A metasynthesis', *Qualitative Health Research*, 12: 453–472.

Bland, C. J., Meurer, L. N. and Maldonado, G. (1995) 'Systematic approach to conducting nonstatistical meta-analysis of research literature (review)', *Academic Medicine*, 70(70): 642–653.

Bondas, T. and Hall, E. O. C. (2007) 'A decade of metasynthesis research in health sciences: A meta-method study', *International Journal of Qualitative Studies on Health and Well-Being*, 2(2): 101–113.

Booth, A. (2006) '"Brimful of STARLITE": toward standards for reporting literature searches', *Journal of the Medical Library Association*, 94(4): 421–429, e205.

Britten, N., Campbell, R., Pope, C., Donovan, J., Morgan, M. and Pill, R. (2002) 'Using meta ethnography to synthesise qualitative research: a worked example', *Journal of Health Services Research Policy* 7(4): 209–215.

Campbell, R., Pound, P., Pope, C., Britten, N., Pill, R. and Morgan, M. (2003) 'Evaluating: Meta-ethnography: A synthesis of qualitative research on lay experiences of diabetes and diabetes care', *Social Science and Medicine*, 56(4): 671–684.

Carroll, S. M. (2004) 'Nonvocal ventilated patients' perceptions of being understood', *Western Journal of Nursing Research*, 26(1): 85–103. February 5, 2009, from http://wjn.sagepub.com/cgi/reprint/26/1/85.

Cooper, H. (1998) *Synthesizing Research*. Thousand Oaks, CA: Sage.

Cooper, H. and Hedges, L. (1994) *The Handbook of Research Synthesis*. New York, NY, USA: Russel Sage Foundation.

Cooper, S. (2002) *Technoculture and Critical Theory: In the Service of the Machine?* London: Routledge.

Crismore, A. (1985) 'The case for a rhetorical perspective on learning from texts: Exploring metadiscourse' (Tech. Rep. No. 342).

Davies, P. (2000) 'The relevance of systematic reviews to educational policy and practice', *Oxford Review of Education*, 26(3–4): 365–378.

Denyer, D. and Tranfield, D. (2006) 'Using qualitative research synthesis to build an actionable knowledge base', *Management Decision*, 44(2): 213–227.

Denzin, N. K. (1978) The research act: An introduction to sociological methods. New York: McGraw-Hill.

Denzin, N. K. (1989) *Interpretive Interactionism*. Newbury Park, CA: Sage.

DeWitt-Brinks, D. and Rhodes, S. C. (1992) *Listening Instruction: A Qualitative Meta-Analysis of Twenty-Four Selected Studies* (Rep. No. Clearinghouse: CS507954), U.S.: Michigan.

Dixon-Woods, M., Booth, A. and Sutton, A. J. (2007) 'Synthesizing qualitative research: a review of published reports', *Qualitative Research*, 7(3): 375–422. Retrieved February 5, 2009, from http://qrj.sagepub.com/cgi/reprint/7/3/375.

Dixon-Woods, M., Cavers, D., Agarwal, S., Annandale, E., Arthur, A., Harvey, J., Hsu, R., Katbamna, S., Olsen, R., Smith, L., Riley, R., and Sutton, A. J. (2006) 'Conducting a critical interpretive synthesis of the literature on access to healthcare by vulnerable groups', *BMC Medical Research Methodology*, 6(35): 1–13.

Doyle, L. H. (2003) 'Synthesis through meta-ethnography: Paradoxes, enhancements, and possibilities', *Qualitative Research*, 3(3): 321–344.

Dubouloz, C. J., Egan, M., Vallerand, J. and von Zweck, C. (1999) 'Occupational therapists' perceptions of evidence-based practice', *American Journal of Occupational Therapy*, 53(5): 445–453.

Duggan, F. and Banwell, L. (2004) 'Constructing a model of effective information dissemination in a crisis', *Information Research*, 9(3). Retrieved January 21, 2009, from http://informationr.net/ir/9-3/paper178.html.

Egger, M., Smith, G. D. and Phillips, A. N. (1997) 'Meta-analysis: Principles and procedures', *British Medical Journal*, 315(7121): 1533–1537.

Estabrooks, C. A., Field, P. A. and Morse, J. M. (1994) 'Aggregating qualitative findings: An approach to theory development', *Qualitative Health Research*, 4(4): 503–511.

Finfgeld, D. L. (2003) 'Metasynthesis: The state of the art-so far', *Qualitative Health Research*, 13(7): 893–904.

Geertz, C. (1973) *The Interpretation of Cultures*. New York: Basic Books.

Glaser, B. G. and Strauss, A. L. (1971) *Status passage*. Chicago: Aldine Atherton.

Glasmeier, A. K. and Farrigan, T. (2005) 'Understanding community forestry: a qualitative meta-study of the study, the process, and its potential for poverty alleviation in the United States case', *Geographic Journal*, 171(1): 56–69.

Glass, G. V. (1976) 'Primary, secondary, and meta-analysis of research', *Educational Researcher*, 5(7): 3–8.

Glassick, C. E., Huber, M. T. and Maeroff, G. I. (1997) *Scholarship Assessed: Evaluation of the Professoriate*. San Francisco: Jossey-Bass.

Gough, D. (2007) 'Weight of evidence: a framework for the appraisal of the quality and relevance of evidence', in J. Furlong and A. Oancea (eds) *Applied and Practice-based Research. Special Edition of Research Papers in Education*, 22(2): 213–228.

Gough, D. and Elbourne, D. (2002) 'Systematic research synthesis to inform policy, practice, and democratic debate', *Social Policy & Society*, 1(3): 225–236.

Hager, W. and Hasselhorn, M. (1998) 'The effectiveness of the cognitive training for children from a differential perspective: A meta-evaluation', *Learning and Instruction*, 8(5): 411–438.

Hammersley, M. and Foster, P. (1998) 'A review of reviews: structure and function in reviews of educational research', *British Educational Research Journal*, 24(5) pp 609–628.

Heaton, J. (2004) *Reworking qualitative data*. London: Sage.

Himam, F. (2002) 'Inventing the future: A meta-ethnographic analysis towards understanding the process of individual and organizational adaptive strategies to change', *ETD collection for University of Nebraska–Lincoln*. Paper AAI3055275. Retrieved January 28, 2009, from http://digitalcommons.unl.edu/dissertations/ AAI3055275.

Hossler, D. and Scalese-Love, P. (1989) 'Grounded meta-analysis: A guide for research syntheses', *Review of Higher Education*, 13(1): 1–28.

Jensen, L. A. and Allen, M. N. (1994) 'A synthesis of qualitative research on wellness-illness', *Qualitative Health Research*, 4(4): 349–369.

Jensen, L. A. and Allen, M. N. (1996) 'Meta-synthesis of qualitative findings', *Qualitative Health Research*, 6(4): 553–560.

Jensen, J. and Rodgers, R. (2001) 'Cumulating the intellectual gold of case study research', *Public Administration Review*, 61(2): 236–246.

Johnson, M. (1999) 'Communication in healthcare: A review of some key issues', *Journal of Research in Nursing*, 4(1): 18–30.

Kearney, M. H. (2001) 'New directions in grounded formal theory', in R. Schreiber and P. N. Stern (eds.) *Using grounded theory in nursing*. New York: Springer. pp. 227–246.

Leshem, S. and Trafford, V. (2007) 'Overlooking the conceptual framework', *Innovations in Education and Teaching International*, 44(1): 93–105.

Light, R. J. and Pillemar, D. B. (1982) 'Numbers and narrative: combining their strengths in research reviews', *Harvard Educational Review*, 52: 1–26.

Lincoln, Y. S. (1995) 'Emerging criteria for quality in qualitative and interpretive research', *Qualitative Inquiry*, 1: 275–289.

Lincoln, Y. and Guba, E. (1985) *Naturalistic Inquiry*. New York: Sage.

Major, C. (2010) 'Do virtual professors dream of electric students? College faculty experiences with online distance education', *Teachers College Record*, 112(8).

Malpass, A., Shaw, A., Sharp, D., Walter, F., Feder, G., Ridd, M. and Kessler, D. (2009) "Medication career' or 'Moral career'? Two sides of managing antidepressants: A meta-ethnography of patient's experience of antidepressants', *Social Science & Medicine*, 68(1): 154–168.

Marshall, C. (1990) 'Goodness criteria: Are they objective or judgement calls?' in E.G. Guba (ed.) *The Paradigm Dialog*. Newbury Park, CA: Sage. pp. 188–197.

Martisen, B., Paterson, B., Harder, I. and Biering-Sørensen, F. (2007) 'The nature of feeding completely dependent persons: A meta-ethnography', *International Journal of Qualitative Studies on Health and Well-being*, 2(4): 208–216. Retrieved from January 21, 2009, from http://www.informaworld.com/smpp/content~content=a777402086~db=all.

McCormick, J., Rodney, P. and Varcoe, C. (2003) 'Reinterpretations across studies: An approach to meta-analysis', *Qualitative Health Research*, 13(7): 933–944.

McDermott, E. and Graham, H. (2005) 'Resilient young mothering: Social inequalities, late modernity and the "problem" of "teenage" motherhood', *Journal of Youth Studies*, 8(1): 59–79.

Morse, J. M. (2001) 'Qualitative verification: Building evidence by extending basic findings', in J. Morse, J. Swanson, and A. Kuzel (eds.) *The Nature of Qualitative Evidence*. Thousand Oaks, CA: Sage. pp. 203–220.

Nightingale, D. J. and Cromby, J. (eds) (1999) *Social Constructionist Psychology: A Critical Analysis of Theory and Practice*. Buckingham: Open University Press.

Noblit, G. W. and Hare, R. D. (1988) *Meta-ethnography: Synthesizing Qualitative Studies*. Newbury Park, CA: Sage.

Pascarella, E. T. and Terenzini, P. T. (1991) *How College Affects Students*. San Francisco: Jossey-Bass.

Pascarella, E. and Terenzini, P. (2005) *How College Affects Students (Vol. II): A Third Decade of Research*. San Francisco: Jossey-Bass.

Paterson, B. L. and Thorne, S. (2003) 'The potential of metasynthesis for nursing care effectiveness research', *Canadian Journal of Nursing Research*, 35(3): 39–43.

Paterson, B. L., Canam, C., Joachim, G. and Thorne, S. (2003) 'Embedded assumptions in qualitative studies of fatigue', *Western Journal of Nursing Research*, 25(2): 119–133.

Paterson, B. L., Thorne, S. E., Canam, C. and Jillings, C. (2001) *Meta-study of Qualitative Health Research. A Practical Guide to Meta-analysis and Meta-synthesis*. Thousand Oaks, CA: Sage.

Pawson, R. (2002) *Evidenced Based Policy: A Realist Perspective*. London: Sage.

Pielstick, C. D. (1998) 'The transforming leader: a meta-ethnographic analysis', *Community College Review*, 26(3): 15–34.

Ponterotto, J. G. (2006) 'Brief note on the origins, evolution, and meaning of the qualitative research concept "thick description"', *The Qualitative Report*, 11(3): 538–549.

Pope, C. Mays, N., Popay, J. (2007) *Synthesizing Qualitative and Quantitative Health Evidence: A Guide to Methods*. London: Open University Press.

Rantala, K. and Wellstrom, E. (2001) 'Qualitative comparative analysis and a hermeneutic approach to interview data', *International Journal of Social Research Methodology*, 4(2): 87–100.

Rice, E. H. (2002) 'The collaboration process in professional development schools: Results of a meta-ethnography, 1990–1998', *Journal of Teacher Education*, 53(1): 55–67.

Richardson W. S., Wilson M. C., Nishikawa, J. and Hayward, R. S. (1995) 'The well-built clinical question: a key to evidence-based decisions' [Editorial], *ACP J Club*, 123: A12.

Ritzer, G. (1992) 'Metatheorizing in sociology: Explaining the coming of age', in G. Ritzer (ed.) *Metatheorizing*. Newbury Park, CA: Sage. pp. 7–26.

Ryle, G. (1968) 'The thinking of thoughts: What is "Le Penseur" doing?', University Lectures, (The University of Saskatchewan) (18). Reprinted in his *Collected Papers*, 2, London: Hutchinson, 1971, pp. 480–496 and in *Studies in Anthropology* (Centre for Social Anthropology and Computing) 11: 1996.

Ryle, G. (1971) *Collected Papers. Volume II Collected Essays, 1929–1968*. London: Hutchinson.

Sackett, D. L. and Wennberg, J. E. (1997) 'Choosing the best research design for each question', *British Medical Journal*, 315(7123): 1636.

Sandelowski, M. (2006) '"Meta-Jeopardy": The crisis of representation in qualitative metasynthesis', *Nursing Outlook*, 54(1): 10–16.

Sandelowski, M. and Barroso, J. (2002a) 'Finding the findings in qualitative studies', *Image: Journal of Nursing Scholarship*, 34(3): 213–220.

Sandelowski, M. and Barroso, J. (2002b) 'Reading qualitative studies', *International Journal of Qualitative Methods*, 1(1) Article 5. Retrieved September 1, 2006, from http://www.ualberta.ca/~ijqm/.

Sandelowski, M. and Barroso, J. (2003a) 'Classifying the findings in qualitative studies', *Qualitative Health Research*, 3(7): 905–923.

Sandelowski, M. and Barroso, J. (2003b) 'Creating meta-summaries of qualitative findings', *Nursing Research*, 52(4): 226–231.

Sandelowski, M. and Barroso, J. (2003c) 'Motherhood in the context of maternal HIV infection', *Research in Nursing and Health*, 26(6): 470–482.

Sandelowski, M. and Barroso, J. (2003d) 'Toward a metasynthesis of qualitative findings on motherhood in HIV-positive women', *Research in Nursing and Health*, 26(2): 153–170.

Sandelowski, M. and Barroso, J. (2007) *Handbook for Synthesizing Qualitative Research*. New York: Springer.

Sandelowski, M., Barroso, J. and Voils, C. I. (2007) 'Using qualitative metasummary to synthesize qualitative and quantitative descriptive findings', *Research in Nursing Health*, 30(1): 99–111.

Sandelowski, M., Docherty, S. and Emden, C. (1997) 'Qualitative metasynthesis: Issues and techniques', *Research in Nursing and Health*, 20(4): 365–371.

Savin-Baden, M. and Fisher, A. (2002) 'Negotiating 'honesties' in the research process', *British Journal of Occupational Therapy*, 65(4): 191–193.

Savin-Baden, M. and Major, C. H. (2007) 'Using interpretive meta-ethnography to explore the relationship between innovative approaches to learning and innovative methods of pedagogical research', *Higher Education*, 54(6): 833–852.

Savin-Baden, M. and Wilkie, M (2004) 'Exploring the impact of discipline-based pedagogy on problem-based learning through interpretive meta ethnography', in M. Savin-Baden and K. Wilkie (eds) *Challenging Research in Problem-based Learning*. Maidenhead: Open University Press/SRHE, pp. 190–205.

Savin-Baden, M., Macfarlane, L. and Savin-Baden, J. (2007) 'Influencing thinking and practices about teaching and learning in higher education. An interpretive meta-ethnography', *Higher Education Academy* http://www.heacademy.ac.uk/projects/detail/lr_2007_savinbaden (Accessed 8 July 2008).

Savin-Baden, M., Macfarlane, L. and Savin-Baden, J. (2008) 'Learning spaces, agency and notions of improvement: Influencing thinking and practices about teaching and learning in higher education. An interpretive meta-ethnography', *London Review of Education*, 6(3): 211–229.

Schofield, J. W. (1990) 'Increasing the generalizability of qualitative research' in E. W. Eisner and A. Peshkin (eds.) *Qualitative inquiry in education: The continuing debate.* New York: Teachers College Press. pp 201–232.

Scholosser, R. W., Koul, R. and Costello, J. (2007) 'Asking well-built questions for evidence-based practice in augmentative and alternative communication', *Journal of Communication Disorders*, 40(3): 225–238.

Schreiber, R., Crooks, D. and Stern, P. N. (1989) 'Qualitative metaanalysis', in J. M. Morse (ed.) *Qualitative nursing research: A contemporary dialogue.* London: Sage. pp. 311–327.

Scruggs, T. E., Mastropieri, M. A. and McDuffie, K. A. (2007) 'Co-teaching in inclusive classrooms: a metasynthesis of qualitative research', *Exceptional Children.* Retrieved January 12, 2009, from http://www.accessmylibrary.com/coms2/summary_0286-32297231_ITM.

Sharpe, R. and Savin-Baden, M. (2007) *Learning to Learn through Supported Enquiry. A literature review conducted for the L2L through supported enquiry FDTL5 project.* Available from http://www.som.surrey.ac.uk/learningtolearn/Resources.asp.

Sherwood, G. D. (1999) 'Meta-synthesis: Merging qualitative studies to develop nursing knowledge', *International Journal for Human Caring*, 3(1): 37–42.

Shkedi, A. (2005) *Multiple case narrative: A qualitative approach to studying multiple populations.* Amsterdam: John Benjamins.

Skrla, L., Scott, J. and Benestante, J. J. (2001) 'Dangerous intersection: A meta-ethnographic study of gender, power, and politics in the public school superintendency', in C. C. Brunner and L. Bjork (eds.) *Advances in research and theories of school management and educational policy: The new superintendency.* Stamford, CT: JAI Press. pp. 115–131.

Stronach, I., Corbin, B., McNamara, O., Stark, S. and Warne, T. (2002) 'Towards an uncertain politics of professionalism: teacher and nurse identities in flux', *Journal of Educational Policy*, 17(1): 109–138.

Suri, H. and Clarke, D. (2009) 'Advancements in research synthesis methods: From a methodologically inclusive perspective', *Review of Educational Research*, 79(1): 395–430.

Taylor, M. C. (1997) 'What is evidence-based practice?', *British Journal of Occupational Therapy*, 60(11): 470–474.

Taylor, M. C. (2000) Evidence-based Practice for Occupational Therapists Oxford: Blackwell Science Ltd.

The Joanna Briggs Institute (2007) The Joanna Briggs Institute Approach to Evidence-Based Practice. The Joanna Briggs Institute. Accessed 27 May, 2007, from: http://www.joannabriggs.edu.au/pdf/about/Approach.pdf.

Thorne, S. (1994) Secondary analysis in qualitative research: Issues and implications, in J. M. Morse (ed.) *Critical issues in qualitative research methods.* London: Sage. pp. 263–279.

Thorne, S. (1998) 'Ethical and representational issues in qualitative secondary analysis', *Qualitative Health Research*, 8(4): 547–555.

Thorne, S., Jensen, L., Kearney, M. H., Noblit, G. and Sandelowski, M. (2004) 'Qualitative metasynthesis: Reflections on methodological orientation and ideological agenda', *Qualitative Health Research*, 14(10): 1342–1365.

Thorne, S., Joachim, G., Paterson, B. and Canam, C. (2002) 'Influence of the research frame on qualitatively derived health science knowledge', *International Journal of Qualitative Methods*, 1(1) Article 1. Retrieved September 1, 2006, from http://www.ualberta.ca/~iiqm/backissues/1_1Final/html/thorneeng.html.

Tickle-Degnen, L. (1999) 'Organizing, evaluating, and using evidence in occupational therapy practice', *American Journal of Occupational Therapy*, 53(5): 537–539.

Walsh, D. and Downe, S. (2005) 'Meta-synthesis method for qualitative research: a literature review', *Journal of Advanced Nursing*, 50(2): 204–211.

Weed, M. (2006) 'Interpretive qualitative synthesis in the sport and exercise sciences: The meta-interpretation approach', *European Journal of Sport Science*, 6(2): 127–139.

Whittemore, R. (2005) 'Combining evidence in nursing research: methods and implications', *Nursing Research*, 54(1): 56–62.

Whittemore, R., Chase, S. K. and Mandle, C. L. (2001) 'Validity in qualitative research', *Qualitative Health Research*, 11(4): 522–537.

Willig, C. (2001) *Qualitative Research In Psychology A Practical Guide to Theory and Method*. Buckingham: OUP.

Zhao, S. (1991) 'Metatheory, metamethod, meta-data-analysis: What, why, and how?', *Sociological Perspectives*, 34(3): 377–390.

Zuboff, S. (1984) *In the Age of the Smart Machine: The Future of Work and Power*. New York: Basic Books.

Glossary

Aggregative An adjective for aggregate, which means to sum existing parts into a whole.

Analysis The process of breaking apart a unit into its component parts.

Audit or paper trail The process of keeping meticulous records of research processes so that they may be documented and replicated in the future.

Coding A system of symbols used to represent themes and concepts.

Conceptual or theoretical framework An existing concept or proven theory that serves to guide study design as well as interpretations.

Confirmability The idea that the researcher has remained neutral in data analysis and interpretation. It is based upon the notion that the researcher needs to demonstrate that results could be and at times even should be confirmed or corroborated by others.

Context When viewing a question or topic, this term means to survey the existing situation or situations in which it is occurring to better understand it as a whole.

Credibility The term credibility is centred on the idea that results are credible and therefore to be believed. It is the idea that the reader can have confidence in the data and their interpretation. The focus is on the trust which can be placed in the accuracy of data and the process by which it was acquired, the sense that it is believable and confidence can be placed in it.

Dependability The notion that the research can be trusted over time. Dependability is derived from the more positivist perspective of reliability and replicability.

Empirical studies Social science studies in which research findings are derived from evidence, rather than simply theory alone. The study, then, whether qualitative or qualitative, involves collecting data in the field.

Evaluative methods Evaluation methods are used to study an organization or curriculum in such a way which contributes to review of policy and decision making within the organization. Thus qualitative methods are used which will enable the researcher and those involved to review the advantages and disadvantages of the programme under study and explore the problems and policies. The classic model used is illuminative evaluation, although there are many others.

Evidence-based medicine   An approach to medical practice in which research is used to inform clinical practice. The intent is to use best evidence for making decisions about patient care.

Evidence-based practice   Evidence-based practice began its development as evidence-based medicine and, as such, began from a very quantitative and 'hard science' perspective. It is currently used to refer to practices in health care that use a range of studies, both qualitative and quantitative to inform the way practices are carried out, thus it is an approach to treatment rather than a specific treatment.

Exclusion criteria   The criteria used to decide which studies will be excluded from the review.

Explanatory literature review   Reviews that explore a particular topic with a view to offering an explanation of the issue under study. These do involve analysis, the form generally is not specified, although at times there is a general mention of 'weight of evidence' criteria, in the sense that if a preponderance of evidence demonstrates a finding, it is considered credible.

Faculty   In the US, teaching/research professionals in institutions of higher education who hold academic rank; used interchangeable with staff in the United Kingdom.

Grey literature   In the context of social science literature, this means those works that do not appear in peer reviewed journals, including conference proceedings, dissertations, etc.

Grounded meta-analysis   Technique for comparing organizational interventions which have been derived from rational-based strategies such as management-by-objectives, planned change.

Grounded theory   A type of qualitative research in which theory is generated from data.

Hand searching   The process of locating articles by hand (often in a library) and checking articles to see whether they are relevant for the review.

Honesties   The idea that there needs to be a sense that what counts as trustworthiness and truth is a negotiated position in research.

Inclusion criteria   The criteria used to decide which studies will be included in the review.

Interpretivism   The perspective that knowledge, contexts, meanings and ideas are a matter of interpretation, thus researchers analyse the meaning people confer upon their own and others' actions.

Iterative   A cyclical procedure that involves revisiting issues, ideas and concerns related to the research.

Literature review   A critical overview of literature in order to identify and make clear the current state of knowledge about a given topic.

Literature summary   the use of research as information, to describe knowledge about a given topic.

Member checking A process for ensuring plausibility in which participants (in the case of synthesis subjects or authors) are contacted to ask whether data interpretations or findings are accurate.

Meta-analysis A process through which statistical methods are used to analyse results from several studies on a given topic, often to determine effect size.

Meta-ethnography An approach to synthesizing and interpreting findings from multiple qualitative studies. Noblitt and Hare (1988), from the field of education, developed this interpretive approach which has served as the basis for most qualitative approaches to synthesizing qualitative research.

Meta-synthesis An approach to synthesis of qualitative studies (or qualitative and quantitative studies) that tends to be aggregative (as opposed to interpretive) in approach. However, the term is sometimes used interchangeably with meta-ethnography.

Naturalisitic inquiry It is research which takes place in the natural setting, sees the researcher as the primary data collecting instrument and is often characterized by the use of an emergent design.

Participant observation Studying people by participating in social interactions with them in order to observe and understand them.

Plausibility A technique for ensuring rigour is qualitative research synthesis that involves locating the truths and the realities in the study, adopting a critical approach and acknowledging the complexities of managing 'truths' in research.

Positivism A philosophical system which recognizes only positive facts and observable phenomena, thus the only reliable knowledge of any field of phenomena reduces to knowledge of particular instances of patterns. Therefore, reality is single and tangible, research is value free and generalizations are possible.

Post-positivism A philosophical approach which argues that realities are multiple, that research is value bound and is affected by time and context.

Practice profession A field that helps to prepare students for work in a particular profession, including education, medicine, law, etc.

Practitioners Those who are employed in practice professions, such as medicine, law, education.

Primary research This term means a process through which a researcher engages in empirical research.

Primary studies Individual studies included in the review referred to in this way before they are synthesized.

Problem-based learning An approach to learning in which students engage with complex, real world situations that have no one 'right' answer, and are the organizing focus for learning. Students work in teams to confront the problem, to identify learning gaps, and to develop viable solutions and gain new information through self-directed learning.

Qualitative research   Describes a developing field of inquiry and that covers several research approaches that share a set of common characteristics. Those who use the approach frequently seek to understand human behaviour. They often are interested in the 'why' and 'how' questions, rather than the 'what'. Data collected and presented generally is thick in its description.

Quantitative research   A field of inquiry that relies upon statistical techniques to analyse data.

Randomized control trials   An experimental study where subjects are randomly allocated to different control groups for the allocation of different interventions.

Reflexivity   Seeking to continually challenge our biases and examining our stances, perspectives, and views as researchers. This is not meant to be a notion of 'situating oneself' as formulaic as pronouncing a particular positioned identity connected with class, gender, race ... but rather situating oneself in order to interpret data demands so as to engage with critical questions.

Research review   The use of a review of research to demonstrate information in a particular way, for example develop a comprehensive picture of knowledge about a topic or issue.

Research synthesis   A standalone report that combines evidence in a way that aggregates information from a body of studies into a new whole.

Researcher bias   The acceptance that in qualitative studies bias exists and is understood as inevitable and important by most qualitative researchers. However processes such as reflexivity are adopted to gain 'a better set of biases'.

Researcher   A person engaged in empirical research, contrasted with a secondary researcher who reviews original data sets to reanalyse and a synthesist who analyses findings from studies.

Saturation   A temporary category, because it is ever evolving, that suggests that once themes are continually repeated, it is no longer necessary to continue sampling to prove the existence of a theme.

Secondary analysis   This process involves reviewing original data sets to reanalyse original data.

Semi-structured interview   An interview process which involves use of interviewing, with an interview protocol that is somewhat set but which also relies on open ended questions to allow for spontaneity of participant.

Social science research   Research within a scholarly discipline designated as a social science, including anthropology, economics, history, psychology, political science, sociology.

Staff   A term used in the United Kingdom to denote professionals who hold rank as lecturers or professors, used interchangeably with faculty in the United States.

Stakeholders   A group or groups of people who have an interest in an issue, institution, or other.

Stance One's attitude, belief or disposition towards a particular context, person or experience. It refers to a particular position one takes up in life towards something, at a particular point in time.

Synthesis The process of reassembling parts into a comprehensive whole.

Synthesist The person who engages in the process of conducting a synthesis of original qualitative studies; we use the term to mark a distinction from researcher, by whom we mean the primary investigators and authors of the studies included in the synthesis.

Thick description Thick description involves explanation of the context as well as the importance of interpretation, thus it is not just reporting detail, but instead demands interpretation that goes beyond meaning and motivations.

Transferability Refers to the idea that findings may be applicable in similar situations. While transferability is generally considered the responsibility of the one who wishes to apply the results into new contexts, the researcher is generally expected to have provided sufficient information about context and assumptions to determine whether the research is transferable.

Transparency Ensuring research processes are documented and presented as rigorously as possible to make the research process clear.

Triangulation The use of different types of methods, researchers and or theories in a study in an attempt to maximize the validity of a study.

Trustworthiness The process of checking with participants the validity of data collected and checking with participants that data interpretations are agreed upon a shared truth. It is evidence of research accountability and involves both integrity and rigour.

Validity Criteria for judging the soundness of qualitative research, thus strategies are developed to ensure there is some kind of qualifying check to ensure the research is sound and credible.

Verisimilitude Demonstrating the appearance of truth; the quality of seeming to be true, which is arguably a more realistic quest than uncovering 'truth'.

Index